FIRE
ON THE
MOUNTAIN

For Jenni—
Thoughtful &
Generous — A Fine
Friend.
Tom

FIRE ON THE MOUNTAIN

EDWARD ABBEY

Perennial

An Imprint of HarperCollins*Publishers*

FIRE ON THE MOUNTAIN. Copyright © 1962 by Edward Abbey. All rights reserved. Printed in the United States of America. No part of this book may be used or reproduced in any manner whatsoever without written permission except in the case of brief quotations embodied in critical articles and reviews. For information address HarperCollins Publishers Inc., 10 East 53rd Street, New York, NY 10022.

HarperCollins books may be purchased for educational, business, or sales promotional use. For information please write: Special Markets Department, HarperCollins Publishers Inc., 10 East 53rd Street, New York, NY 10022.

First Avon trade edition published 1992.

Reprinted in Perennial 2003.

Library of Congress Cataloging-in-Publication Data is available.

ISBN 0-380-71460-4

03 04 05 06 07 RRD 10 9 8 7 6

For Rita

The story which follows was inspired by an event which took place in our country not many years ago. However, it is a work of fiction and any resemblance to living persons or actual places is accidental.

FIRE ON THE MOUNTAIN

Brightest New Mexico. In the vivid light each rock and tree and cloud and mountain existed with a kind of force and clarity that seemed not natural but supernatural. Yet it also felt as familiar as home, the country of dreams, the land I had known from the beginning.

We were riding north from El Paso in my grandfather's pickup truck, bound for the village of Baker and the old man's ranch. This was in early June: the glare of the desert sun, glancing off the steel hood of the truck, stung my eyes with such intensity that I had to close them now and then for relief. And I could almost feel the fierce dry heat, like that of an oven, drawing the moisture from my body; I thought with longing of the cool water bag that hung from the hood latch over the grille in front, inaccessible. I wished that Grandfather would stop for a minute and give us time for a drink, but I was too proud and foolish to ask him; twelve years old, I thought it important to appear tougher than I really was.

When my eyes stopped aching I could open them again, raise my head and watch the highway and fence and telephone line, all geometrically straight and parallel, rolling forever toward us. Heat waves shimmered over the asphalt, giving the road far ahead a transparent, liquid look, an illusion which receded before us as fast as we approached.

Staring ahead, I saw a vulture rise from the flattened carcass of a rabbit on the pavement and hover nearby while we passed over his lunch. Beyond the black bird with his white-trimmed wings soared the western sky, the immense and violet sky flowing over alkali flats and dunes of sand and gypsum toward the mountains that stood like chains of islands, like a convoy of purple ships, along the horizon.

Those mountains—they seemed at once both close by and impossibly remote, an easy walk away and yet beyond the limits of the imagination. Between us lay the clear and empty wilderness of scattered mesquite trees and creosote shrubs and streambeds where water ran as seldom as the rain came down. Each summer for three years I had come to New Mexico; each time I gazed upon the moon-dead landscape and asked myself: what is out there? And each time I concluded: *something* is out there—maybe everything. To me the desert looked like a form of Paradise. And it always will.

The shadow of the vulture flashed by on the right.

Grandfather put his big freckled hand on my knee. "See the jack rabbit, Billy?"

"Yes sir. That's number ten. Ten dead jack rabbits on the road since we left El Paso."

"Well, that means we're almost home. They average about one dead rabbit every five miles. This year. Now ten years ago you could drive all the way from Baker to El Paso and see maybe one rabbit."

The old man, crouching under the roof of the cab, squinted through his spectacles at the road unpeeling ahead, like a seam on the world. Seventy years old, he drove at seventy miles an hour. In that flat and empty land such a speed seemed leisurely. He crouched because the roof of the truck was too low. The truck, almost new, had a cab wide enough to accomodate four men but not high enough for one. Part of the trouble was Grandfather's hat, which was one foot tall, but he could not take it off because that would be immodest. So he spread himself laterally as much as he could, putting his left elbow and shoulder out the window and his right arm across the top of the seat.

The steering wheel he controlled with the tip of his left forefinger.

"A rabbit is a kind of rat, Grandfather."

"I've heard about that. And we haven't looked at the whole thing, either. This system benefits the vulture, as we noticed a minute ago. It helps preserve the balance of nature. Over-all efficiency, I call it. We also have efficient overalls. Did you bring yours?"

"Yes sir." I looked out the rear window to make sure my suitcase was still in the bed of the truck. It was there, my leather companion all the way from Pittsburgh.

"You'll need them," the old man said. "We got work to do tomorrow. You and me and Lee, we're going up on the mountain tomorrow, gonna look for a horse and a lion. How does that sound?"

"That sounds wonderful, Grandfather. Lee's coming too?"

"He said he'd come."

A glow of pleasure spread through my nerves. I hadn't seen Lee Mackie for nine months—the nine months I'd spent imprisoned in school back East—and I missed him. I could never imagine a finer man than Lee; when I thought of him I knew what I wanted to be when I grew up. I wanted to be Lee Mackie II.

"Will we see him today? Is he out at the ranch now?"' As I looked at Grandfather, waiting for his answer, I hooked my arm around the gallon jug at my side, our gift for Lee, which we had selected that morning in the market place of Juarez. There was another jug beside it, Grandfather's gift for himself. And on my feet were brand-new boots with built-up heels and toes sharp enough to kick holes in door panels, the first genuine cowboy boots I had ever possessed.

"He said he'd try to get out there sometime tonight. Your Lee's a busy man these days, Billy. He's got himself a wife now, and a broker's license, and a real estate office, and a big fat automobile with four headlights and six taillights and three hundred and fifty horsepower. He's got big ambitions. You won't recognize him anymore, Billy."

I paused to consider this information. "I don't care," I said. "Lee can handle anything. Besides—I knew he was going to get married. He warned me last year about that. We talked it over and I said it would be all right this time."

The old man smiled. "Just so it don't happen again, is that the idea?"

"Yes sir."

"Well, you won't see so much of him this year. But he's promised to come out to the ranch as often as he can anyway, so don't feel discouraged." And he gave my shoulder a gentle squeeze. "Stick with me, Billy. We're in for a lively summer. I'm gonna need you, boy."

I took a deep breath, swelling with pride and resolution. "I'm ready for anything, Grandfather. Trouble or anything." I opened the dashboard compartment and peeked inside: half-concealed beneath papers, matches, snakebite kits and tools was the old revolver in its leather case.

"But you keep your eager little paws off that gun. If I ever need it I don't want to have to go a-searching for it under your pillow. You hear me, Billy?"

"Yes, sir." I felt a flush of embarrassment on my cheeks. The summer before I had borrowed the revolver, without telling the old man, and kept it on my bed at night.

"Don't you worry about it," he said. "We'll have some target practice tomorrow. I guess you're old enough now to start learning how to handle a gun."

"Sure I am, Grandfather." I thought about that, staring ahead at the endless highway. We straddled another dead jack rabbit. "Grandfather, did you ever shoot anybody?"

The old man paused before replying. "Not yet," he said.

"Did Lee ever shoot anybody?"

"Well—you ask him. He was in the war. Ask him sometime, he'll tell you all about it. I think he got some kind of a medal. You'll have to prod him a little. Not much."

"A medal for shooting people?"

"Well, it was the war. Absolutely legal. Tell me what you did in school last year."

"Nothing, Grandfather. I graduated. Next year I'm going away to school. They're sending me to a prep school."

"You think you'll like that?"

"Dad's always telling me what a lot of money it will cost so I guess I'd better like it. He wants me to be an engineer. Mom wants me to be a doctor."

"What do you want to be?"

"I don't know, Grandfather. I'd like to stay here with you and Lee. I think I'd like to breed horses."

"Maybe you should have been a horse."

"Sir?"

"I'm kidding you, Billy." He played with the new straw hat on my head. "How does the hat feel?"

"All right, only it's kind of stiff."

"We'll break it in." After a moment he said: "You be patient with your folks, Billy. They want to do all they can for you."

"Yes sir."

"Why, how many parents do you think would let their boy travel all the way across the country by himself to spend the summer with a crazy old man? Did you ever think about that?"

"Yes. I know. I only wish—they wouldn't be so nervous about it. They get so nervous about everything."

"That's what you call an occupational disease. There's no cure for it. Watch the cows and the hens, they get the same way. It's all part of nature's infernal plan."

"All part of what, sir?"

"Nature's eternal plan. Look at that!"

A road runner broke from the brush and streaked across the highway before us, beak and neck and tail stretched out above invisibly racing legs. Once across, the bird vanished into the scenery, leaving behind a trace of smoke.

"Now there's an interesting case for you," Grandfather began. "The road runner—the cuckoo of the desert. Now he could fly across the road if he really wanted to. Be a lot safer. But he won't do it. Too doggone stubborn. He'd rather risk his neck than give up his rights. What can you do with a bird like that?"

"Maybe the jack rabbits are the same way, Grandfather."

"No, the jack rabbits operate on a different principle—they don't take chances, they commit suicide. They jump right into your headlights, eyes wide open. No pride, no dignity and no brains. The road runner takes a sporting gamble but he knows what he's doing and never gets hit. He's a solitary bird, he has to think for himself. The rabbit doesn't have that problem."

Something changed in the appearance of things to the north. Where the highway merged with horizon there now rose up, quite suddenly, a water tower labeled B and a string of blue smoke, a cluster of bright green cottonwood trees and the square shapes of houses and store buildings. We passed an automobile graveyard and an abandoned gas station ("Save 2¢"), a scatter of tarpaper shacks, a hard new motel, supermarket and cafe, and slowing down rapidly, entered the village of Baker. Grandfather's ranch lay twenty miles due west, near the foot of the mountains; we were almost home.

The old man parked the truck in front of Hayduke's place, a combination general store, post office, and bus stop. When he turned the motor off the silence was startling; the only sound I could hear at first was the rattle and groan of a jukebox in the bar next door. A little weary, we climbed out of the truck and stood in the fierce glare of the sun. I reached for the water bag on the front of the truck.

"How about some soda pop?" the old man said. I nodded. "Come on in the store."

We walked into the cool gloom of the interior, where I had to pause to allow my eyes to readjust themselves.

"Fix the boy up with a bottle of pop," I heard my Grandfather say.

"Yes sir, Mr. Vogelin!" And the sprightly figure of the storekeeper took shape in the darkness before me, a bottle opener in his hand. "Howdy, Billy. Glad to see you back. You just open that cooler over there and help yourself. No charge."

"Thank you," I mumbled.

"Any mail for me?" Grandfather asked.

"You got a couple more of them Government letters back here somewheres," Hayduke said, ducking into the little fourth-class post office walled into one corner of the store. "Yes sir, Mr. Vogelin, I seen them this morning. Somewhere back here . . . hold on a minute . . . yes sir, here they are. That's the one from the Corps of Engineers and this here one's from the District Court. How's everything going, Mr. Vogelin?"

I found the cooler and opened myself a bottle of root beer, took a deep drink and looked around for the toilet. A long drive, from El Paso to Baker. "You know as much about that as I do," I heard Grandfather say as I walked to the door I needed. "And here's a dime for the soda pop."

"That's twelve cents now, Mr. Vogelin, unless you're leaving the bottle here."

"We'll take the bottle with us, Hayduke."

Grandfather was waiting for me outside in the heat, the pop bottle in his hand, when I came out. "Here you are, Billy." The letters stuck out of his shirt pocket, unopened. "Come on next door and we'll have a beer."

As we started to walk away the Greyhound bus came in, bound for Albuquerque from El Paso, and stopped for a moment in front of the store, where the driver blew his horn and threw a bundle of newspapers onto Hayduke's porch. No passengers got on, none got off; the bus roared onward into the north, Alamogordo next stop, thirty miles away. I gripped my bottle firmly and tightened the hat on my head as we stepped into the vast and shady vacancy of the Wagon Wheel Bar. Men had died in this place.

A little withered cowboy squatted on top of one of the bar stools, watching us enter, blinking as we let in a blast of fresh air and sunshine.

"Close that door, John," he said to my grandfather. "Now look at them flies. What's it like out there? Still hot?"

"Go out and see for yourself," my grandfather said. He ordered a can of beer from the Mexican behind the bar.

"I go out when the sun goes down," the little cowboy said, hunkered on top of the stool. Like an Indian, he'd never learned properly how to sit on a chair. "Hello, Billyboy," he said to me, "what're you a-doin' in this corner of Hell? Why ain't you in school where you belong?"

"It's June," my Grandfather said. "Vacation time. Billy's come to spend another summer with us at the Box V. If you ever went outside in the daylight, Bundy, you'd learn to tell the difference between winter and summer."

"Winter," the little cowboy said, peering thoughtfully up at the ceiling. "Summer. Oh, I remember what they're like, John. I seen 'em both one time."

"Well, have another look," Grandfather said; "they need you out there."

The Wagon Wheel was a good bar. I'd always liked it—roomy, gloomy and quiet, always cool even on the hottest days of July and August. Best of all I liked the mural on the windowless east wall, a great primitive picture twenty feet long and ten feet high showing Thieves' Mountain against an immaculate blue sky and three ragged black buzzards circling above a horseman in the heart of the White Sands. The horse trudged over the dunes with hanging head and closed eyes. The rider sat slumped in the saddle, a dark stain of blood on his shirt, the shaft of an arrow sticking out of his back, and a rifle hanging loosely from his limp left arm. The artist had given the painting a title: "Desert Doom, or Forty Miles From Hope."

I drank my root beer and studied the picture, while Grandfather carried on a sullen talk with the little cowboy.

"I hear you declared war on the United States Government, John," the cowboy said.

"No, they declared war on me."

"Maybe the Government needs more help." The little man paused and said: "Whose side is Lee on?"

"I think he's on my side."

"Well, maybe the Government will need more help. I think maybe I oughta volunteer, lend 'em a hand. When the summer's over, I mean, and it ain't so god-awful hot outside. You think I should join the Army, the Navy, the Marines or the Air Corpse, John?"

"Bundy, you're giving me a headache." The old man finished his can of beer and turned to me. "Let's go, Billy."

Grandfather and I stepped outside into the scalding brilliance of the afternoon. The heat was like the blast of a furnace, but the dry air sucked the sweat from my body and gave me at least the illusion of comfort. We made for our truck, with its Box V brand painted on the door panel, and climbed in. After a stop at the new supermarket on the edge of town, where the old man bought some flour and beans, we drove south to the turnoff and headed west over the twenty miles of hard-riding dirt road that led to the ranch.

The landscape before me was much the same as that in the mural on the wall of the Wagon Wheel Bar. To the west rose the broken tooth of Thieves' Mountain, the peak ten thousand feet above sea level, adorned with a feather of cloud. North were the San Andres Mountains, with the white dunes of gypsum flowing for fifty miles along the base of the range, and to the south were the Organ Mountains, tapering off into the dimness and emptiness of the borderland and Old Mexico. Even the buzzards were present, two of them, hovering high in the blue, meditating on space, but the savage eyes missing nothing that stirred in the desert below—belly, beak and claws taut with hunger and desire. Next turn around, I thought, if we get the choice, I too want to be a long-winged, evil-minded predatory bird.

We came to the boundary and then to the gateway of my grandfather's little kingdom. He stopped the truck, I got out, slid back the drawbar of the gate and swung it open. Above my head, hanging from the cross-pole of the gate frame, a weather-silvered board inscribed with the Box V brand creaked on its iron rings. The old man drove the pickup through, I closed and latched the gate, and climbed back to my seat.

We drove on across the salt flats of an ancient lakebed, where the heat shimmered up in palpable waves. Through the layers of heat and light I watched the dislocated outlines of the mountain ranges flow together, floating on a yellow sea of haze. In that country, fantasy and mirage were always present.

After the lakebed we passed clay hills with the shape of giant beehives, turrets and ledges of sandstone, and a wild garden of yuccas with stems ten feet tall. The road slipped into a broad wash, we churned through the soft hot sand and up the other side through thickets of willow and tamarisk, where a group of the old man's bald-faced Herefords lay shaded up, waiting for the sun to sink before they'd rise and resume the search for something to eat. The cab of the truck filled with fine dust, a layer of it coating the dashboard, where I wrote my name with my finger: BILLY VOGELIN STARR.

We didn't try to talk much during the drive, with the truck bouncing like a bronco, the motor roaring, the bitter alkali getting in our eyes and teeth. Grandfather stared straight ahead from under the brim of

his grimy hat and clutched at the bucking wheel; I
kept looking all around, feeding my eyes and mind
and heart on the beauty of that grim landscape. Hard
country, the people call it. A cow might walk half a
mile for a mouthful of grass, and five miles for a drink
of water. If the ranch had been mine I'd have sold the
cattle and stocked the place with wild horses and buf-
falo, coyotes and wolves, and let the beef industry go
to ruin.

We topped the final rise and won our first view of
the ranch headquarters, a mile ahead and a thousand
feet below. There was the grove of cottonwood trees
surrounding the ranch-house, the windmill and water
tank, and the cluster of sheds, corrals, barn, bunkhouse
and other outbuildings nearby, all spread out on a
bench of land above the arid bed of what was called
the Salado River, where a trickle of hard water me-
andered from one bank to the other.

Grandfather stopped the truck, shut off the motor,
and sat for a while staring down at his home, a sad
and perplexed expression on his wind-burned leathery
face.

"Everything looks the same as ever, Grandfather,"
I said. "Like it did last year and the year before. The
way it should."

He stirred, champed on the cigar, reached over and
put his big hand, his gripping machine of bone and
muscle and hide, on my shoulder. "I'm mighty glad
you're here, Billy. Stay awhile this time."

At that moment I was ready to forsake my other
home, forsake my mother and father and little sister
and all my friends, and spend the rest of my life in
the desert eating cactus for lunch, drinking blood at
cocktail time, and letting the ferocious sun flay me
skin and soul. I'd gladly have traded parents, school,
a college education and career for one dependable
saddle horse. Later that night, of course, alone in bed,
the deadly homesickness would strike me faint.

"Sir, if you'll let me, I won't go back. I'll never go

back. I'll stay here and work for you for the rest of my life."

The old man laughed. "You're a good boy, Billy." He squeezed my shoulder. We gazed down at the ranch for another minute or so, then Grandfather raised his arm and pointed toward Thieves' Mountain. "That's where we'll be tomorrow. Looking for that pony. We'll spend a night at the old line cabin and I'll show you some lion tracks." He turned the ignition key and started the engine. At the same time I saw the contrails of three jet planes coming out of the north and blazing white across the clean clear blue of the sky. I pointed to them. "Three jets, Grandfather. See them, way up there?" More beautiful, I thought, even than vultures.

The old man didn't share my sentiment. "Trespassers," he muttered, the smile fading from his face. His good humor had vanished again. We talked no more on the drive down to the ranch. Parking the truck under the trees, Grandfather walked in silence toward the house, ignoring the dogs that leaped at us, barking with happiness. Wolf, the big German police, leaped on my chest and lathered my face with his wet tongue, and a couple of pups I'd never met before galloped and rolled around us like idiots.

Everything looked and smelled and sounded marvelous to me: the fat trees with their trunks like the legs of gigantic elephants and their masses of translucent, quaking acid-green leaves; the windmill clanking and groaning as it turned in the breeze and pumped good cold water up out of the rock; the saddle horses snorting at the water trough in the corral; the milk cow bawling and the hens squawking; the sound of an angry baby howling over in the mud hut where the Peralta family lived. Best of all was the sight of the ranch-house with its massive walls of adobe brick and its small square windows like the gunports of a fortress.

We climbed the steps onto the long verandah, passed under the rack of buckhorns and the horseshoe, and entered the cool dark interior of the house. At once

I smelled the familiar fragrance of simmering pinto beans, of chili sauce and fresh-baked bread, and knew I was home again.

Through the gloom of the parlor, advancing to meet us, came Cruzita Peralta, Grandfather's cook and housekeeper. Plump, brown as saddle leather, handsome, Cruzita cried out with delight when she saw me and embraced me as she would a child of her own, half-smothering me against her ample and pneumatic bosom.

"Billy," she said, "it is so good to see you. My how big you get in just one year, now you come up to my neck, eh? Soon you be big and tall like a real man, taller than your grandfather. Only not so ugly, I think. Give me another kiss, my Billy. I bet you are hungry, no? Such a long trip, all by yourself, like a big man."

I managed to struggle free of her entangling arms and admitted that I was hungry, that I would like something to eat.

"You better take care of your baby, first," Grandfather said. "He's awake again. Then come back and feed this boy. He ain't had nothing to eat since we left El Paso."

Cruzita rushed out of the door and trotted through the sun-spangled shade of the trees toward her own house. The old man and I moved through the darkness toward the kitchen, where he fixed me up with a tall glass of ice water and mixed himself a highball of ice, rum and water. Stirring his drink, he sat down at the table and invited me to do the same. The long drive across the desert had burned us dry. Refreshed but tired, we sat in silence and waited for the woman to come back.

I poured myself a second glass of water from the pitcher and looked around, sucking on the ice cube in my mouth. All looked the same as ever: black pot of beans on the stove, a row of pans hanging on the wall, geraniums in tomato cans on the window sill, the big stainless-steel refrigerator and freezer, which worked on bottled butane, standing in the alcove beside the stove, where the old man had placed them years before. He had no use or need for electricity, but he did like ice in his drinks. The refrigerator, the pickup truck, and the disposable toothpick, he confessed, were the three great achievements of modern man.

Cruzita returned, the baby in her arms, which she placed on the floor away from the stove before serving Grandfather and me each an overflowing plate of fried beans, fried beef, fried eggs, and fried potatoes, all liberally spiced with red chili sauce. With the plates came thick slices of her new-baked bread, and butter, jam, milk, and coffee. With a good appetite I ate the meal I'd been anticipating for a day and a half and nearly two thousand miles on the train. As I ate I wiped the tears from my eyes, blew my nose, drank all the water and milk in sight, and added an extra touch of hot sauce to my beans.

Finished, unwrapping a fresh cigar, Grandfather leaned back in his chair, tilting it against the wall. "Where's Eloy?" he asked. Meaning Eloy Peralta, Cruzita's husband and the old man's hired hand.

Cruzita poured him another cup of coffee. "He say he go to the north line, Mister Vogelin. He want to fix that break in the fence below the cinder cone, where the jeeps come through."

The old man growled. "Yeah, them soldier boys. By God, if they do that once more I'm gunning for them."

"What happened?" I asked.

Grandfather gave me a brooding stare, looking at something inside his head. The expression softened. "Well, Billy, they like to hunt jack rabbits, you see, these here soldiers from the Proving Grounds. They got nothing else to do, I guess, so they go barreling after the crazy scared jacks and bust right through my fence. Second time this year. You might think if they want a war so bad they could find one overseas somewhere and leave us citizens in peace." He lit the cigar and partially disappeared behind a fog of gray smoke.

From outside, the lowing of the milk cow reached our ears. Cruzita was washing the dishes and rinsing them off with boiling water from the kettle on the stove. "That cow," she said, "always wants milking when I'm busy. Let her wait."

"She'll jump the fence," Grandfather said.

"I finish these dishes first, damn cow."

"Maybe the calf got out. Ain't that calf weaned yet?"

"Two more weeks," Cruzita said.

The cow bawled again. With a clatter of noise she stacked the dishes in the drying rack, scooped up the baby from the floor, and bounced out of the kitchen. The old man and I watched her go.

"Cruzita can do most anything, can't she, Grandfather,"

"She's a good woman. She sure has spoiled me. How she can manage to look after all those kids and Eloy and the cow and the hens and me too is something I'm kind of afraid to ask about." He puffed slowly on his cigar and stared at the dark ceiling through skeins of smoke. His own wife had died fifteen years ago in the hospital at Alamogordo. Watching his old and saddened face, I wondered if he was thinking now about that. I knew that something deep was troubling his mind. I wanted to ask but also knew that when he wanted he would talk to me about it.

The dark and stillness of twilight was filling the room: sun going down beyond the barren snag of the mountain.

Grandfather rose from his chair. "Let's go out on the porch, Billy. Eloy should be tracking along now."

"When's Lee coming, Grandfather?"

"I don't know for sure; sometime tonight, he said."

We pushed open the screen door of the kitchen and stepped out on the long verandah, which enclosed and shaded the west and south walls of the house. Great spokes of sunlight radiated into the sky above Thieves' Mountain, gilding the undersides of the fleet of small cumulus clouds, clear and definite in shape, which floated there on one invisible plane of air. Close by, blue-black and stark against the sunset, the nighthawks swooped upward and then plunged like bullets through the swarms of insects hovering above the cattle trails along the wash. Bats flickered through the twilight around the corral and water tank, making a strange noise that always reminded me of the crackling of a bad electrical connection. The Mexicans of the South-west had the custom of catching a bat when it was asleep during the day and nailing it, alive, to the barn door in order to frighten away *las brujas*—the witches. There are plenty of witches in New Mexico, some good, some bad, all unreliable and all with a weakness for fooling with other people's livestock. I didn't be-lieve in witches myself—but I knew they were there.

"Here comes Mr. Peralta," I said, as a horse and rider appeared at a walking pace from out of the wil-low groves along the almost-waterless river. Eloy Peralta, Grandfather's only full-time ranch hand, was a good man, good at anything worth doing, and willing to work about 364 days a year for $150 a month, plus room and board for himself and family. He was being exploited, of course, but perhaps didn't know it, or if he knew it, didn't care. He seemed to enjoy such things as stringing barbed wire, shoeing horses, branding calves, and arguing with my grandfather, and when he got mad and quit, as he sometimes did, he knew he could always come back the next day.

"I quit!" he roared as he came toward us through the gloom on the tired, lathered horse. "Gee-whiz Christ and bloody Mary!" He checked the horse by the porch steps and looked at us. A grin flashed in his saddle-colored face when he saw me. "Billy-boy! Wel-come back to the worthless and burned-up and eat-out-no-good-run-down Vogelin drag strip." He pulled one foot from the stirrup, eased his short leg up and rested it on the neck of the horse. The horse, old Skilletfoot, reposed on his bones, switching his tail at the gnats and letting his head hang down between his forelegs. I returned the greeting. There was a short silence as Peralta stared at the sunset and picked sandburs off his pants leg.

"Better go home and eat your supper, Eloy," Grandfather said. "I don't want to hear about it right now."

Peralta grunted in disgust. "No, you don't want to hear about it. Listen, Meester Vogelin, I think we better go someplace else, maybe New York, Pennsyl—what's that place, Billy?—Pennsylvania, okay? I don't want to work on no bloody drag strip no more."

"Go home and eat and shut up," Grandfather said wearily.

"Sure, okay, shut up. Maybe we shut our eyes too, huh? That might help." He picked at the burrs on his jeans. "Today they were not chasing the jacks, Meester Vogelin."

"No? What were they chasing?"

"I don' know. What was it? I don' know. A thing long and white and shiny, come down like an arrow and start to burn up. Three jeeps and the men in the yellow tin hats, they all race after it, hey! like crazy men."

"Did they tear up that fence again?"

"Fence? No, I fix that. No, they find the gate this time and leave it open, one two three cows get out. All the afternoon I hunt these three cows. When I try to talk to the wild men they make me stay away from where they are, they run the jeep at me and scare the horse and scream at me to stay away, stay away!" Peralta imitated the men in the yellow tin hats, waving his arms and howling quietly. "Stay away! stay away! you dirty Mexican."

"Did they call you that?"

Peralta hesitated. "I think so."

"What did you call them?"

Peralta hesitated again, glancing at me. "I don' call them nothing, the dirty gringos. Maybe they hear me, I don' know. I go away, hunt the cows. Then the big truck comes with the red lights and the siren, like this."

He tilted back his head, removing his hat, and howled gently at the sky, like a siren. He stopped. "Tomorrow we maybe find the cows."

"Eloy, you shouldn't talk like that in front of the boy."

"I know and I am very sorry."

"Go home and eat. Get off that poor horse. God, look at his feet, he's cast two shoes again."

"Meester Vogelin, I cannot keep shoes on this hammerhead. We need the frying pans, I think."

"We need a bullet," Grandfather muttered. Peralta waved at me, grinning, and started toward the corral, with a cloud of gnats doing their molecular dance around him and his mount. "Tell Cruzita I'll fix up the boy's room," the old man yelled after him, and Peralta nodded.

"You and me better get some sleep, Billy," Grandfather said. "We'll be leaving before sunup tomorrow."

We took my luggage and the grits out of the pickup and re-entered the house. The old man led me through the enormous main room with its Indian rugs on the floor, past the cavelike fireplace where a stack of mesquite logs awaited kindling, under the antique rifles and game trophies mounted on the walls. Beyond the living-room we passed Grandfather's office. The door was open. I caught a glimpse of the rolltop desk piled high with papers, ledgers and letters. On top of the desk stood photographs of the old man's wife and his three daughters: my mother, living in Pittsburgh; Marian, living in Alamogordo; and Isabel living in Phoenix. All married, with children and problems of their own. Above the desk was an oil portrait of Jacob Vogelin, Grandfather's father, the somber bearded Dutchman who had founded the ranch back in the 1870's by first defrauding and then fighting off the Mescalero Apaches, the Southern Pacific Railroad, the Goodnight Cattle Company, the First National Bank of El Paso, and the United States Government with its never-ending wars, depressions, and income taxes.

Past the office we followed the dark carpeted hallway which led to the bedrooms. The first two were closed; the third was open and we walked in. This was the same room I'd slept in during the two preceding summers but in the meantime the daughters had been using it during the occasional visits to Grandfather. The room bore the feminine stamp of their occupancy—flowered wallpaper, pink and pastel-green bedspreads, brocaded drapes and ballerinas' *tutus* hanging over the windows, shutting out the light and air.

We stopped just inside the doorway, looking around. "Do you like this room, Billy?"

I paused, then said, "It's very pretty."

"Does it give you a sort of suffocated feeling?"

"Yes sir."

We were silent. "Tell you what," he said, "you sleep here tonight. After we get back from our ride in the mountains we'll clean up one of them rooms in the old bunkhouse, chase out all the vinegaroons and scorpions and sidewinders and fix you up proper. What do you think of that?"

"Yes sir."

"What?"

"I think that's a good idea, Grandfather."

"Fine. That's what we'll do. Now let's have a look at one of these here woman's beds." He turned back the corner of the green coverlet and discovered fresh sheets, smelling of soap and wind and sunshine, already laid. "Good old Cruzita, she's been here before us. God bless her sweet heart." A quilt lay over the foot of the bed. Grandfather unfolded it and spread it over the bed. "All right, Billy, you get your clothes off and get in bed and tomorrow we'll—head for the hills. How long since you been on a horse?"

"Nine months."

"Nine months? Yes, you better get some sleep." He started to leave, but stopped by the kerosene lamp on the dresser. "Want me to light this lamp for you, Billy?" The room was half dark.

"No, Grandfather, I don't need it."

"Fine. Did you wash your face and brush your teeth?"

"Yes."

"When?"

"This morning on the train."

Grandfather thought for a moment. "Fine. Well— good night, Billy."

"Goodnight, sir."

He went out, closing the door. Alone in the silence and darkness, aware of the strangeness of the room and the land I was in, I felt the first pang of homesickness. But instead of brooding over it I undressed, setting my new straw hat carefully on the bureau and lining up my new boots on the floor at the foot of the bed. Tired but unable to sleep, I opened a window and watched the sickle of the new moon floating in the west, and listened to the bullfrogs croak—to my ears a song sweeter than that of any nightingale.

Eventually I crawled into bed and lay there with my hands under my head, looking up at the dim ceiling. Another spasm of loneliness struck through me as I remembered home and my mother, who by this time would be tucking the covers around me and kissing me on nose, forehead and mouth before going downstairs. I found that I missed that familiar ceremony, missed it painfully, and when I felt something wet slide over my cheekbone I knew I was crying. For a while the shame of my tears overcame my nostalgia and I fell asleep. Fragments of dreams floated through my brain—the head of my horse plunging up and down as we climbed into the foothills, a black man grabbing my shoulder as I loitered in the vestibule of the roaring train, the clash of human voices in argument.

Waking again, I remembered hearing a car or truck drive up to the ranch-house. My grandfather's voice, solemn and bitter, brought me wide awake. I sat up in bed, listening. The sky through the window was brilliant with stars.

The old man stopped. I heard the tinkle of glass and ice and the distinct gurgle of liquid poured from a bottle with a narrow neck, then the quiet voice of another man, also familiar—the voice of Lee Mackie.

Spurred by a sudden excitement, I slid out of bed and listened hard but could not make out what was being said. Putting on my underwear I stepped to the door and opened it, quietly, and peeked down the hallway toward the living-room. The glass eyeballs of a stuffed antelope reflected the glow from a lamp; light wavered softly over the octagon barrel and silvery breech of the old .45 carbine cradled in the antelope's horns. From where I stood I could see neither my grandfather nor Lee. But I could hear them clearly and what I heard quelled my original impulse to rush down the hall to greet my friend.

"Now listen carefully, old horse," Lee was saying. "You know it won't do any good at all to get fired up about this and declare war on the Benighted States of America. They got you where the hair is short and that's all there is to it and you might as well make the best of it—I mean, take the sixty-five thousand."

"The Box V is not for sale!" Grandfather thundered. A pause: I heard the old man's sigh and a bang as he brought the glass down hard on the table, before bursting out again. "The Box V is not for sale. The Box V never was for sale. The Box V never will be for sale. And by God no pack of brass hats and soldier boys and astro—astronauts or whatever you call 'em is gonna take it away from me. I'll die first. No—they'll die first. Why I never heard of such a thing. Every citizen of Guadalupe County, every mother's son in New Mexico, should be loading his guns right now."

"Don't talk foolish, John."

"I mean it."

"Don't yell at me."

"I'm not yelling. You're yelling."

"You're hollering like a bull. You'll wake the kid."

A brief spell of quiet followed that remark. Lee spoke

again, so gently that I had to step a few paces down the hall to hear. "You think any of these scum around here will stand with you, John? Do you? Don't believe it."

"Reese'll go along with me. And Haggard maybe. You'll go with me."

"Me? What can I do, John? Listen, you know what the men in town think about this? You know what the Chamber of Commerce thinks about this?"

"I know, I know. They think—"

"They think this business'll make 'em all rich. Richer. And they think you are loco. Senile, that's the word, they think you're just a crazy old man in his second childhood. And they'll think worse than that too, if you know what I mean. Obstructing national defense. You against one hundred and eighty million Americans."

"There ain't that many. There can't be."

"Well there is. And they're busy making more right now."

"Well—they're all back East somewheres. No kin of mine."

"They're all against you. At least they're not with you. That goes for Reese and Haggard too; they'll sell out without any trouble, you wait and see."

"You're with me."

"I'm with you. But—"

"The boy is with me."

"Billy is with you. But that's—"

"Three men can stand off about a million of these— what do you call 'em—astro, astronauts."

"Astronauts. Yeah. But they have the papers and the law. They have Acts of Congress, national emergency, eminent domain, right of condemnation, declaration of taking. What do you have?"

"What do I have?" My grandfather's voice soared up again. "I have the land. My ranch. No government in the world is going to take it from me."

A moment of silence. "I really ought to go home,"

Lee said. "Poor Annie waited up for me till twelve last night."

"You're not going anywhere. You're staying right here tonight. I told the boy you'd be going with us tomorrow. How do you think he'd feel if you . . ."

"I know, John. I was only talking. I didn't haul that horse fifty miles just for the ride, did I?"

I stood awkwardly against the wall of the hallway, half-naked and shivering, one foot going numb and my knee aching. I wanted very much to see Lee before I went back to bed. On the other hand I did not want them to know I had been overhearing their talk. Though what I'd heard seemed unbelievable anyway. Unable to decide, I shifted my position a little to relieve my stiffened limb. In the night silence the old man heard the movement.

"Billy?" he said. I gulped, unable to reply. "That you, Billy?" I heard the creak of a chair and Grandfather appeared in the doorway at the end of the hall, his glasses shining and his white mane aglow with the soft yellow night from the lamp. "Why aren't you in bed?"

"I wanted—I wanted to say hello to Lee," I mumbled.

And all at once there he was, looming up behind the old man and smiling at me. Lee Mackie, tall and slim and dark-eyed, a brave and gallant man. "Hello, Billy," he said. He held out his right hand. "It's good to have you back, Billy. You come down here and say hello."

2

Wake up!
Hey, dude, wake up!

Dreams evaporating, I felt a rough hand shaking the bed, opened my eyes and saw in the starlight the laughing face of Lee Mackie. I sat up at once, charged suddenly with excitement and a wild delight.

His eyes gleamed in the darkness. "You awake?"

"Yes. Yes," I said.

"Get dressed. Come and eat. We're taking off for the mountain in ten minutes."

I slid out of bed and stood up shakily, rubbing my eyes. Through the window I could see the stars in unfamiliar constellations glittering like diamonds on the deep-velvet sky, a spray of stars so clear and bright they seemed no farther away than the leaves of the trees.

"Here, I'll light the lamp for you." Lee felt for matches in his pocket, found them, struck fire and lit the wick of the kerosene lamp on the dresser. "How many eggs, Billy? Three or four?"

"Four." I looked for my suitcase. The clothes I wanted were inside it.

"Hurry up. We'll give you one minute to get dressed." Lee backed off through the doorway and tramped away down the hall, whistling like a mockingbird.

I opened the suitcase and pulled out my blue jeans and the tight cowboy shirt with the diamond-shaped imitation-pearl buttons—a great shirt. The air was chill; I dressed quickly, tugged on my boots, grabbed my new hat and hobbled out and down the hallway toward the warm glow of the kitchen.

Lee stood bent over the rumble of fire in the cookstove, stirring a mess of eggs and potatoes in an oversize iron skillet. Flame and smoke leaked out around the edge of the skillet—the stovelid had been shoved aside. The redolence of burning juniper graced the air. Lee heard me approach and greeted me with his white grin, nodding toward the table, where three places had been set. I went first to the sink, turned the tap, and splashed cool water over my face. I dried my face with the fresh towel that hung on a handy nail, combed my hair with my fingers, and was ready.

"Get your grampaw in here," Lee said. "We're ready to eat."

I went to the screen door and called the old man. He stood outside on the bare ground below the verandah, talking with Eloy Peralta, two dim figures in the morning dusk. Grandfather dismissed Eloy with a clap on the shoulder and came into the kitchen. We three sat down at the table and ate, by the light of the lamp, the hot and hearty breakfast Lee had made. I was hungry, beautifully hungry, with an appetite I'd almost forgotten I'd ever had.

"That's the way to shovel it down," Lee said, grinning at me enthusiastically. "Look at this boy eat, John. You can always tell a cowboy by the way he eats. If he don't eat like a wolf there's something wrong with him."

The old man smiled at me. "We'll keep him." His huge left hand was clamped around a mug of steaming coffee; I could see the freckles and the red hair on his knuckles.

"Have some more, Billy." Lee scraped more of the scrambled eggs and fried potatoes out of the skillet onto my plate. I added a few extra slices of bacon from the second frypan and buttered another slab of bread. "That's the idea," Lee said. "Man, if we find that lion today, I sure feel sorry for the lion."

"Or suppose he finds the horse before we do," Grandfather said. "That's a valuable horse."

"Nature's plan," I said through a mouthful of food. They watched me eat.

"Let's go," Lee said, as I finished. "I can feel the sun coming up over Texas." He gulped down the last of his coffee, pushed back his chair and stood up, reaching for his hat. I stood up and reached for my hat and when Lee put his on I put mine on.

Grandfather unwrapped a cigar. "Be right with you boys. Don't wait for me."

Lee strode outside and I followed. Parked near the verandah was Lee's enormous custard-colored automobile, gleaming with chrome and glass. He stroked its sleek enamel as we passed. "Some piece of iron, huh Billy?"

"It's a nice car, Lee," I didn't really pay it much attention; where I came from the streets were more or less solidly paved with these metallic objects and a man on foot could walk across a street only when the machines permitted him to. They were as familiar to me as the feel of soot on cement and the smell of sewer gas. My father leased two new ones every year.

We walked quietly through the gloom under the shivering leaves of the cottonwoods toward the barn and corral. I saw the green ribbons of dawn stretched out above the purple mesa eastward. A horned owl hooted from the willow thickets. Meadow larks and canyon wrens, invisible but present, sang out clear as angels in the pasture beyond the corral and in the alfalfa field along the wash.

"Lee," I said.

He gripped my arm for a moment. "Let's not talk about it today, Billy. It'll be all right. Don't let it worry you."

The screen door clapped shut behind us, a loud noise in the stillness, and glancing back I saw the red coal of the old man's cigar as he came down the steps of the porch.

Lee and I entered the barn, felt our way into the tackroom and loaded ourselves with gear. Lee filled a feedbag with grain and we stepped out of the barn into the corral. Holding a bridle behind my back, I looked at the group of horses stamping and snorting in the far corner of the corral, hungry but worried. To me, in that half light, they looked big as mastodons, their eyeballs flaming with red menace, their hooves pounding like sledges on the hard earth.

Lee handed me the feedbag. "Choose your mount."

I advanced slowly toward the huddled animals, feeling scared and made even more scared by my effort not to show it. I looked for my favorite, a small buckskin gelding with black mane, broomtail, long legs. This was the horse I had most often ridden the year before. I couldn't make him out in the shifting mass of horses.

"Where's Rascal?" I asked.

"Rascal?" Lee said. "Why Billy, that's the one we're hunting for today. He's been missing for a week."

My grandfather came out of the barn with a saddle on his shoulder. "Take old Blue there, Billy. He's the one you want now."

I stepped forward again, holding out the bag of grain, and now the horses came to meet me and crowded close, thrusting their muzzles at the feedbag, shoving me toward the fence and stepping carelessly on my new boots. I offered the bag to Blue, a big gray, draped the reins around his neck and led him out of the mob and back to the corral fence. While the horse ate his breakfast I climbed part way up the fence and laid the saddle pad and the saddle over his broad back.

I no longer felt any fear. The massive bulk of the animal, his powerful jaws crunching bran and barley into gruel, his docile indifference to my activity, inspired me with confidence and affection. I was foolishly proud of the fact that such a great strong beast would submit to my purpose—at least when bribed. I cinched the saddle as tight as I could and climbed aboard to

test the stirrup lengths. Too long: I had to dismount
and readjust them. By this time Lee and the old man,
pretending not to observe my efforts, had their own
mounts saddled, bridled, fed and ready to go.

Blue was nearly finished. I tried to take the feedbag
away from him so that I could get the bit in his mouth.
He shook his head, hurling me to the ground. I got up,
waited respectfully until he was satisfied there was
nothing more in the bag, then bridled him successfully
and climbed up into the saddle.

The world looked different from up there—better.
A primitive joy flowered in my heart as I guided the
horse away from the rails and toward the gate. A touch
of my heels and he walked forward; a slight tug on the
reins and he stopped. I leaned forward and rubbed the
mighty shoulders. "Good old Blue . . ." I felt about ten
feet tall, a master of horses and men. The wild birds
crying in the desert echoed the delight of my soul.

Lee and Grandfather came alongside, Lee on a dark
quarter horse, Grandfather on his big sorrel stallion,
Rocky. Grandfather said, "You ready, Billy?"

"Yes sir!"

"Tie this on your saddle." He gave me a poncho,
smiling at me. He faced the east; I saw reflections of
the dawn on his glasses. I didn't understand at first why
he was smiling at me in so strange a way, until I felt
the tears welling out of my eyes. "Do you feel all
right?"

"Yes sir." I looked away. "Grandfather, I—I'm
so . . ."

"I know, Billy. I know how you feel." He caressed
my back. "Let's go."

Lee moved ahead and opened the corral gate, dis-
mounting and remounting with his usual practiced ease.
We rode through, leaving the gate open, and the remaining horses followed us. When we broke into a
brisk trot down across the irrigated field toward the
river of sand, they halted and watched us go, heads up
in solemn curiosity. I felt sorry for them, left behind.

At that moment I would have felt sorry for anyone in the world, man or beast, who was not going with us.

When we reached the west gate, Grandfather got down and opened it and we passed through; he closed the gate and drew up beside us as we rode through the willow and tamarisk bordering the wash. *El Rio Salado.* The salty river. We rode across the firm sand and gravel, coated with white alkali, to the narrow channel of water shining with motion on the far side. We stopped there for a few minutes, allowing the horses a final drink before heading into the desert and arid hills beyond.

I watched a pair of sandpipers scamper on twinkling legs beside the water, upstream, and became aware of the quiet rustle of multitudes of leaves overhead. I stared up at the boughs of the cottonwoods on the bank above us, their leaves caught in a fantastic silvery pre-dawn light and fluttering continuously, though I could scarcely feel the breeze. Alive, the trees whispered in soft excitement, enjoying the best hour of the day. The sun when it rose would force them into somnolence through the withering heat of forenoon and afternoon. I knew how they felt and how they could feel.

"Kit fox," Lee said.

I looked hurriedly around, searching the high ground for a glimpse of a fox.

"Down here," he said, pointing to the mud near the water.

I looked hard and discerned the tiny doglike tracks coming down to the stream.

"I'm glad to know there's still a few of them left," Grandfather said. "They ain't poisoned them all, yet."

The horses raised their heads. We jogged them forward, splashed through the shallow current, climbed the bank where it was broken down by the passage of many cattle, and moved through the grove of trees and up the gravel mounds beyond the river bed to the open range. Ahead of us lay a five-mile expanse of sand, stone and cactus, then the foothills dotted with juniper and pinyon pine which led up to the mountains and the bald summit of Thieves' Peak.

The gramma grass, dried out to a tawney brown, grew in little circular clumps under the brush, among the boulders and sand dunes. There was no other grass. The cattle, who went everywhere, ate what they could find but did not and could not depend on this sparse growth for life. They browsed on the tough shrubbery of the desert—the black-brush, chamisa, cliffrose, ephedra, greasewood and mesquite. In hard times, in desperate times, the cattle would even eat the prickly-pear cactus, sometimes helped by the rancher who went before them with a flame-thrower and burnt off the thorns. If this was not enough the rancher would have to buy feed. If he went broke buying feed he could then sell his stock and wait for rain and a better year. If the rain delayed too long he sold his ranch or let the banks take it away. The smaller the ranch the greater the risk, and my Grandfather Vogelin was one of the few independent ranchers who somehow had survived the wheel of drouth and depression. He seldom broke even but he didn't break.

We rode beneath a giant yucca in full bloom, a kind of monstrous lily with a base of leaves as big, rigid and sharp as bayonets, a stalk twelve feet tall and a panicle of fat white waxy flowers. Scattered across the desert in all directions stood more of these solitary, flowering scarecrows.

"Look at that thing," Grandfather said. "You know, a man came out to see me one day, said he was from the Range Management Bureau. He saw these here yuccas and he asked what they were good for."

"What'd you tell him?" Lee said, grinning at me.

"I'm a patient old fool," Grandfather said. "I tried to humor this fella. I told him the Indians made baskets out of the leaf fibers, used the stalks for fences and shade, and made good medicine out of the flowers. Always saving plenty of yuccas for future use, of course. But the man said to me, We got paper and cellophane and cardboard now, who needs a basket? He said, You don't need shade now, you go indoors and turn on the air conditioner when it's hot. And he said, As for medicine, you get all you need in Juarez for five dollars a gallon."

"I think he had you there," Lee said.

"He won the argument," the old man said, "but he lost his immortal soul. So he tells me this and he asks me, What is the yucca good for? How could I answer a question like that? I know how the yucca feels about it but I couldn't put it into words any more than a yucca can. I couldn't say it holds the soil down—there ain't no soil here. I couldn't say it casts a welcome shade—it won't shade a rabbit. Well, he saw he was pushing me into a corner and he made his big play. The yucca is not good for anything, he says. It drinks your water and it eats the minerals in your ground but it doesn't do you one—one nickel's worth of good. What should I do about it? I asked him. Kill them, he said; kill every—every horny one of the ugly things. And don't stop there, he said; look at those cottonwood trees along the wash, sucking your river dry. What can I do about that? I asked. Ring them, he said. They're bleeding you like vampires—cut them down. Think of the awful waste. Don't you believe in conservation? he asked."

"He was threading you like a needle," Lee said. "What did you say to that?"

"I said yes sir, I believe in conservation, and he said, Then do something about it or someday we'll revoke your grazing permit, make you eat cottonseed cake and TV dinners."

"Like everybody else," Lee said. "Looks like he was making cutlets out of you."

"He sure was," the old man said.

We rode on quietly for a few long moments. "What did you do, Grandfather?" I asked.

"I'm ashamed to say I lost my temper. But I made him bleed in the irrigation ditch so none of the valuable fluid was wasted and I planted the body by the bunkhouse door, where you might have noticed those hollyhocks growing so straight and vigorous. The ones with the big pink flowers. The next day a young fella from the National Fish and Wildlife Service came out to see me, wanted to show me a new type of gun—a cyanide gun for exterminating coyotes, foxes, mountain lions and other meat-eating predatory species of animals."

"How did the cyanide gun work, John?"

Grandfather dropped the stub of his burning cigar on a passing anthill. "It worked very well."

"You can't stop progress."

"No, they got around me. Now they just fly over the country in an airplane and drop tallow balls everywhere. The wild animals like them. Maybe children do too, I don't know."

"Tallow balls?" I asked.

"Meatballs," Lee explained, "loaded with Ten-Eighty."

"If you don't know what that is," Grandfather said, "you'll probably get a chance to taste some someday. It's a wonderful new kind of poison that works through a whole chain of animals. It kills the first animal that eats it, kills the animal that eats the first animal, kills the animal that eats *him*, and so on down the line. Of course the poison gets diluted as the victims pass it along so I suppose we'll end up eventually with buzzards too fat to fly and maggots too bloated to crawl."

"That's progress," Lee said. "You can't deny that."

"That's what I'm afraid of," Grandfather said. "Progress. I say, Let's turn back the clock. Why does progress have to progress over me and the coyotes?"

"Well, you've heard of the Juggernaut. When missiles get bigger, missile testing ranges have to get longer."

The old man frowned; he didn't want to talk about that. Changing the subject, he said:

"Close your jaw and open your eyes and look at

that mountain." He raised an arm and pointed toward the granite of the high peak, now glowing with light from the rising sun.

"Why do they call it Thieves' Mountain?" I asked, staring up at the transmutation of bare gray rock into gold.

"It belongs to the Government," Grandfather said.

"Yes, the Government stole it from the cattlemen," Lee said. "And the cattlemen stole it from the Indians. And the Indians stole it from the—from the eagles? From the lion? And before that—?"

"—Before that?"

"Look," Grandfather said proudly, "see how the light comes down the mountain now. Rolling toward us like a wave."

Old man, proud of his mountain. I looked where he pointed. Swiftly and smoothly the sunlight was spreading downward from the peak to the crest of the lesser mountains north and south, down over the belt of pine to the juniper and pinyon stands of the foothills. Bands of light extended across the green sky, passing above us from the east, expanding from the fiery core that swelled below the rim of the world. Turning in the saddle I looked for the sun and in a moment the first arc of it appeared, then more until the entire fireball rose, dazzling and incredible, more beautiful than thought, above the Guadalupe range eighty miles away.

"Yes," continued Lee, "like a wave. But whose light? whose mountain? whose land? Who owns the land? Answer me that, old horse. The man with title to it? The man who works it? The man who stole it last?"

The sun blazed on our backs as we rode toward the mountain, Grandfather's mountain, and the shadows we cast stretched out before us, grotesquely exaggerated, miles long, folding over rock and shrub and prickly pear and crescent sands, clear to the foot of the hills. Flocks of sage sparrows swirled like dark confetti ahead of us, chirping mildly, and off to the left in the shadows of the brush a covey of Gambel's quail ran off obliquely from the path of our advance, making their piteous little cries.

"I am the land," Grandfather said. "I've been eating this dust for seventy years. Who owns who? They'll have to plow me under. My God, I forgot my cigars."

"Brains full of sand," Lee grumbled, cheerfully. "Arrogant as a bull. Head screwed on backwards."

"Every man has his faults, *politico*."

We came to a fence, the west boundary of the old man's deeded property. Beyond this line began the hills and the mountains which my grandfather and his father had used as summer range for ninety years but which belonged, in the legal sense of the word, to the Federal Government. Grandfather held the land now on lease within the complicated provisions of the Taylor Grazing Act. The land on the other side of the fence did not, however, reveal in any way its legal status: it was rocky and dry and sunny and almost though not quite worthless—it looked perfectly real and natural. You could never have guessed, looking at it, that it belonged to the United States of America and was colored a uniform green on maps.

There was also a gate, which my grandfather had built and maintained, and which it was my turn to open. I opened the gate, led my horse through, and closed the gate after the old man and the young man rode through. A great number of dead tumbleweeds lay banked against the fence; also a few immaculately white, sand-scoured cattle bones, the little that remained of the victims of a remote and almost forgotten blizzard.

We rode on, the hills much closer now. The individual junipers that grew on the northern slopes of the hills looked bigger but no clearer, no more distinct, than they had looked from five miles away. The air in that country, except when the wind blew, was of a startling clarity, filled with nothing but light, oxygen, and the promise of lightning. Good for breathing and seeing.

Directly ahead of us a canyon came down and parted the hills and spread a delta of sand and rocks over the plain. Near the mouth of this canyon stood a corral and a windmill and a tank full of water, where a small herd of cattle with wet muzzles waited, observing our approach. Each animal wore on its left flank the brand of the Box V, and all of them, including the little calves, watched us intently, like deer. No horse was up there. We stopped.

"Before we do anything else," Grandfather suggested, "before they shy and mess up the trail, let's cut sign clear around that bunch and see if that pony's been down here."

"Do you think the lion might've got him?" I asked.

"No."

"A lion's mighty lucky to catch a full-grown horse," Lee said. "Even a scatterbrain like Rascal."

"Rascal's not scatterbrained," I said.

"How would you phrase it?"

"Will a lion attack a man?" I asked.

"What for?" Grandfather said.

"The meat."

Lee grinned at me. "A lion will never attack a man unless the lion is too old or too sick to catch decent game. Or unless the lion is cornered, or angry, or wounded, or bored, or curious, or very hungry, or just plain mean."

"Thank you," I said. "That answers my question."

"Are you gentlemen ready to proceed?" Grandfather asked.

"We are."

"Then meet me about one hundred and eighty degrees from here." He started off to the right in a big circle that would take him around the windmill and around the cattle, examining the ground as he went. Lee moved off to the left; I followed Lee.

"What are we looking for?" I asked.

"Tracks. What are you looking for?"

"Trouble."

"You're a hard customer, Billy Starr. But you came to the wrong country. People out here don't like trouble. They don't even like people. That's why they live out here."

I stared up at the hard and silent hills; the rocks would soon begin to bake. "Why do you live in Alamogordo, Lee? Don't you like it out here anymore?"

He studied the sandy desert floor ahead as the horses ambled forward. "Cow and calf. Whiptail lizard. Road runner. More cows. No horse. Raven. Another lizard. Little birds. Cow and calf. Coyote. Everybody comes down here for a drink."

"Why, Lee?"

He kept his eyes on the ground. "Why, Billy? A man gets ideas, Billy." He spoke slowly and gently. "Sometimes he wants to do something—something big. He wants to play a part in things, have something to say about the way things go—and grow. Sure I liked it out here—I loved it. But ten years is a long time. The world is changing, Billy. Your grandfather don't like to admit it but the world is changing. And even New Mexico is part of the world now. You'll know what I mean, Billy, pretty soon."

My heart sank a little as I listened to those quiet words—they had a knell-like tone. I had no answer for them.

Lee halted his horse and looked at me, his dark eyebrows arched at a quizzical angle, his expression kindly but serious. For a long moment he gazed at me with that grave, disheartening seriousness on his face; then his dark eyes lit up again, warm and gay, he broke into that flashing smile, reached out and thumped my back. "Hey, buddy, get that funeral look off your face! Cheer up and smile. The end of the world's still a long way off." He watched me steadily until my face began to reflect his contagious humor. "There, that's better—my God, Billy, for a minute you looked exactly like one of those shoe clerks up in Albuquerque. Now come on, let's join up with the old man."

We started up our horses again, completed our half of the circle without finding any sign of Rascal, and met Grandfather on the far side of the windmill. "Well," he said.

"No sign," Lee said.

"No, I didn't expect we'd find any. He's still up there in the hills, somewhere, damn his ornery nature. Let's go tank up on water and then we'll make tracks for the sky."

We turned and rode slowly toward the windmill. The heat was rising; already I saw the first whirlwind standing up out in the desert, a pillar of dust that spun crazily for a few seconds, crashed into a giant yucca and collapsed. I was thirsty enough to smell the water.

"I see one sick calf in that bunch," Lee said, uncoiling his rope and shaking out the loop. The cattle began to move.

"Somebody build a fire," the old man said wearily. "I was afraid of this."

I recognized an order when I heard it; much as I needed a drink, I dismounted on the way to the tank to pick up twigs and dead sticks for kindling. While Lee went galloping after the cow and her calf and Grandfather drew a running iron and the vaccine syringe out of his saddlebags, I opened my knife, pared shavings from a stick and lit a little fire. Grandfather placed the tip of the iron in the fire, opened his own knife and tested the blade's edge with his thumb. I led old Blue to the tank, watered him and tied him to the corral fence; at the same time Lee came back to the fire dragging the calf at the end of his rope. Beside the calf came the mother cow and both of them were bawling.

I preferred not to watch what was going to happen. I leaned over the wall of the steel tank, which was already hot from the sun, took off my hat and submerged my head in the cool water. Under the water's surface I opened my eyes and peered down through green mystic depths to where tadpoles undulated dreamily among clouds of algae.

Coming out for air, I turned my head for a look at the struggle. Through the dust I saw Grandfather kneeling on the trussed-up calf, the blade glinting in his hand, and saw Lee drawing the white-hot iron out of the fire. The bellow of cow and calf were deafening; I went under water again.

The next time I came up the operation was over: branded, castrated, earmarked, de-horned and inoculated, the calf had staggered on trembling limbs back to its mother. But something was wrong: the old man sat on the ground in the meager shade of the corral fence, sweating, his glasses off, and Lee was fanning his face with a hat.

"I tell you I'm all right," my grandfather snarled. "Give me back my hat." And he reached out, snatched it from Lee's hand, and smashed the hat down on his head.

"You sure you're all right?" Lee was saying.

I ran up to them. "What happened?"

"Your grandfather—"

"Nothing happened," Grandfather roared, though his face shone with sweat. "A bellyache, that's all. I'm okay now, just let me get my breath, will you?"

"I think you better—"

"Lee, will you stop fussing over me?" the old man pushed himself up on his knees and from there to a standing position. He brushed the dust from his pants and felt around for his glasses. "Now where in the devil—"

"Here, here." Lee put the glasses in his hand.

"Thank you." The old man drew the bandana from his hip pocket, wiped the glasses carelessly and put them on. "All right. Let's get a drink of water and get out of here." He walked heavily toward the tank, muttering and grumbling. Lee and I looked at each other.

"Maybe he ate too much chili last night," Lee said, shrugging his shoulders. "That's what he claims."

"I don't know," I said. "You think he's all right now?"

"Maybe. He seems to be mad enough."

Grandfather raised his dripping face from the water, wiped his mouth on his sleeve, untied his horse and swung briskly into the saddle. Without a word to us he started up the rough trail road that led into the mountains. We stared at him. He checked his horse and glared back at us. "Well—? You two coming or do I have to do everything myself?" We climbed on our mounts and rode hastily after him.

"Nice day," he said as we all drew abreast on the narrow road. "But hot. It'll be good to get up yonder." He squinted at the crest above, the line of granite against the deep dark delirious blue. Not even a shred of cloud could be seen in that vibrant sky.

"We'll split up when we reach the south ridge trail."

"Sure," said Lee.

"Keep your eyes peeled from here on, Billy."

"Yes sir."

I looked intently about. The vegetation changed as we gained elevation, the brush of the desert yielding place to parks of pinyon pine and juniper and thickets of shiny green scrub oak. I could smell the sweet scent of resin and pine needles, and heard, from somewhere up ahead, the excited clamor of flocks of pinyon jays. I saw a redheaded woodpecker dart through the air and land on a dead and lightning-blasted jackpine. Some of the juniper trees stood decked out in showers of tiny berries the color of turquoise; I plucked a berry and bit into it—hard, bitter, the flavor of turpentine—or gin. I spat it out. My shirt was beginning to stick to my back; I pulled the tail out and let it hang free.

We rode on, climbing higher. Sweat dripped through my eyebrows and burned in my eyes. My rump ached as the heavy pounding climb of the horse jarred my bones and tender seat. I was getting hungry and wondered though did not dare ask when we would eat lunch—what lunch? Worse than that, I was already thirsty again. I should have drunk a lot more water when I had the chance, I thought, visions of the green pool below the windmill passing through my mind. I should have drunk it all, tadpoles, crawdads, algae and all, when I had the chance.

Lee and the old man rode a pace ahead of me on the narrow trail, giving me all the benefit of the dust. I screwed up my courage: "Did anybody bring any water?"

"A bellyfull," said Grandfather.

"I mean, a canteen."

Grandfather and Lee looked at each other in mock astonishment. "Did you hear that?"

"I heard it but I don't believe it."

"I can't believe I heard it even."

"Listen," I said, "I'm thirsty."

"Maybe he's right," Lee said to Grandfather. "After all, the Campfire Girls always carry canteens. The Boy Scouts always carry canteens. Maybe he's right."

"I'm serious," I said.

"I thought you said you were thirsty."

"I'm serious and thirsty. I'm seriously thirsty. Besides, the United States Cavalry always carried canteens."

"That's because they were always lost," Lee explained. "If you don't know where you are or where you're going it might help a little bit to carry a canteen. If you don't have to depend on it. If you are lucky enough to find water even though you are lost. Why if it hadn't been for the the movies the United States Cavalry would *still* be lost. They'd have lost the war."

"What war?" Grandfather said.

"Why—the war they won."

"What war was that?"

"Let's forget it," I said. "Let's forget the whole thing."

We arrived now at a place high on the hillside where

a dim little trail forked off to the left. The wagon road we were following continued on up the hill in the general direction of Thieves' Mountain. Grandfather halted his horse and looked around. He looked back at the sun. He looked at me and Lee. "I'll take the ridge trail," he said. "You boys keep to the road. I'll meet you at the cabin this evening."

"What do we do if we find the horse?" I asked.

Grandfather studied my new straw hat. "How does the hat feel, Billy?"

I touched the brim. "Pretty good, Grandfather."

"Does it keep your head cool?"

"Yes sir."

"Not too cool?"

"No sir." I loosened the hat a bit.

"Not numb?"

"No sir."

"Good." He touched his spurs to the big sorrel and started up the side trail. He stopped between a pair of tall jackpines. "Come here for a minute, will you, Billy?" He looked at Lee. Lee nodded and moved on up the wagon road. When I reached my grandfather Lee was hidden from us by the trees. "Come close, Billy," the old man said. He looked again to make sure that Lee could not see us, then opened one saddlebag and pulled out a war surplus canteen, U.S. Army model. "I was only kidding you about the water, Billy." He unscrewed the cap and handed the canteen to me. "Take a good swig of that." He smiled as he watched me drink. "Pretty good, huh?"

I drank a little more and gave the canteen back to him. "Yes sir," I said. It was good hot well water, the best I believe I had ever tasted.

"Why a man's a fool to run around out here without any water a-tall," Grandfather said. He took a short drink and put the canteen back in the saddlebag. "Only don't tell Lee, will you, Billy?"

"I won't, Grandfather."

"You promise?"

"I promise."

"Fine." He patted me on the shoulder. "And if you find that pony, just put a rope on him and bring him along. Okay?"

"Yes sir."

"Fine. Now you join up with Lee. Don't let him get lost. I'll see you this evening." He turned the big horse and jogged away from me, up the winding path toward the crest of the ridge, and was soon out of sight among the pines.

I trotted old Blue down the path to the road and caught up with Lee, who was standing beside his horse. "Everything all right?" he said.

"Sure. He's all right."

Lee looked back down the road to where the trail forked off. "He went on up the trail?"

"Yes."

Lee grinned at me. "You still feel thirsty, Billy?"

"No, not much."

"I know what you mean." Still grinning, Lee unbuckled a saddlebag and drew out a military-style canteen. "Have a little water, anyway."

We each had a pretty good drink before Lee put the canteen away. "Your grandfather is a great man," he explained, buckling the saddlebag cover, "the finest man I know. But you know how these old-timers are— kind of stubborn in their ideas sometimes. Too proud to admit they might be wrong about something."

"A man's a fool to run around out here without any water a-tall."

"That's the truth, Billy. Only—don't mention this to him." Left hand on the pommel, ready to mount, he looked at me: "What do you say?"

"I won't breathe a word of it, Lee."

"That's my buddy." He swung himself up to the saddle. "Now let's move on out and see what the mountains have been doing when we weren't around to help."

The mountains had been doing a lot. They were

doing very well. The stones and boulders, sparkling with veins of feldspar and quartz, looked bright and clean and solid in the sun, fresh enough to eat on, as new as if created yesterday. The junipers smelled sweetly, the jackpines stood tall and frankly perpendicular, and the pinyon pines had boughs heavy with clusters of green gummy seedcones, a bumper crop of nuts that would ripen through the summer and be ready for harvest in September. Among and above the trees flew a lively traffic of bluejays, finches, magpies, canyon wrens, phoebes, mockingbirds and woodpeckers, with a few big blue-black ravens croaking here and there, and above all this, about one thousand feet higher, a solitary hawk floating on a thermal column of air. The flowers, too, were rising between the ruts of the road and out of cracks and thumbholes in the boulders and in all the open spaces among the evergreens—the purple larkspur, the scarlet bugler, the golden beeweed, the blue and pink penstemon, the pale yellow sand verbena and the bright red Indian paintbrush. Also a few scattered yuccas, much smaller than the giants of the plain below, some of them in blossom and some dead. I broke off the slender stalk of a dead one and carried it like a lance, resting the butt on my stirrup tap. Sgt. William Starr, United States Cavalry, advancing toward the stronghold of the Mescalero Apaches, accompanied only by a single scout.

"Try to keep that thing out of my eyes, Billy."

"I'm sorry." I transferred the lance to the off-side.

"Thank you. Tell me, Billy, can you hear what I think I hear?"

"What do you mean?"

"Let's stop." We stopped. "I think," Lee said, "I think I hear a jeep."

We listened hard. I could hear nothing but the heavy breathing of the horses, the squawk of a raven, the light and quiet breathing of the trees. "I don't hear it."

"I don't either, now," Lee said, "but I did a minute ago."

We listened again, And this time we both heard it, the whining of a jeep engine in compound low, coming around a bend far up in the hills. Coming toward us.

"How did they get there?" I asked. "They didn't go up this way." No tracks on our road.

"I know. They must have come by way of that old mine road to the north that goes through the reservation."

"Reservation? What reservation?"

"The military reservation. White Sands. The rocket range."

"Oh." I thought about that.

"Let's go on."

We rode on, keeping the horses at a fast walk up the winding and ever-ascending road. It was the kind of road that only a jeep could negotiate—a sensitive and agile jeep.

Within a mile, at one of the narrowest points on the narrow road, with the slope of the mountain rising steeply on one side and falling steeply on the other, we met the visitors. The open jeep crawled down the pitch with motor groaning, brakes squeaking, wisps of steam leaking from under the front end of the hood. Lee and I halted, blocking the road. The jeep had to stop, and as soon as it stopped, the engine stalled. The man at the wheel cursed and began grinding on the starter; the overheated motor balked. We could smell the gasoline flooding over the carburetor as the driver pumped on the gas pedal. After a moment he gave this up, stopped pumping, and looked at Lee across the lowered windshield of his vehicle.

"Hello," Lee said.

"Get the hell out of my way," the driver said.

Lee paused to consider the implication of this greeting. There were three men in the jeep: the driver, the man at his side, and the man in the back seat. All three wore Army fatigue trousers, sweaty T-shirts, Army fatigue caps. They looked tired. The man sitting beside the driver held a double-barreled shotgun upright between his knees; the man in back held some sort of high-powered rifle with telescopic sights in one hand and a half-empty fifth of whisky in the other. The jeep was an Army jeep, olive drab, with identifying markings on the bumper and the hood. Lashed to one of the front fenders with the slim, silver-gray, beautiful and dead body of a coyote.

"Hey, look what we got here," the man with the shotgun said, smiling broadly. "We got two real cowboys. One big cowboy and one little cowboy. On real horses, just like real cowboys. What do you know about that."

"I see you've been hunting," Lee said, addressing all three of them, since all three appeared to be in about the same condition. Almost as strong as the smell of gasoline was the smell of the whiskey, radiating from the men like the heat waves from the hot hood of the jeep. "I wonder," Lee went on, "if you happened to see a horse."

"We're not looking for a horse," the driver said. "We got a jeep. Get the hell out of my way."

"We killed that coyote," the man in back said, grinning. "Easy." He raised the bottle to his mouth.

"Congratulations," Lee said. "The horse we're looking for is a buckskin—"

"Hey you," the man with the shotgun said. "Big cowboy . . ."

"—is a buckskin gelding with a black—"

"Are you for real?" the man with the shotgun interrupted again. "Are you a real cowboy?"

Lee paused. "Sure he is!" I shouted. Lee glanced at me and motioned me back. I stayed where I was, wondering if Lee had a gun hidden in his saddlebags. Not that it could do him much good now. I kept a tight grip on my yucca lance.

The man with the shotgun smiled at me. "Jesus Christ," he said, "we got two of them. The big cowboy and the little cowboy. This is too much. This is getting out of hand."

"Get out of the way," the driver said. He eased up on the brake pedal and let the jeep roll slowly forward until the front end was almost under the head of Lee's horse. He stopped. "I said get the hell out of the way." His radiator sizzled.

"Certainly," Lee said. "As soon as one of you answers my question."

"We didn't come out here to answer questions," the man in back with the high-powered telescopic-sighted rifle said. "We came out here to kill things." He grinned; he had power clutched in each fist. The rifle lay across his legs, pointing at nobody, but his right hand was on the pistol-grip stock and his forefinger inside the trigger guard.

"That's right, big cowboy," the man with the shotgun said. And he raised the shotgun a little and aimed the two big blue barrels at Lee's chest. "Now you just back your horse off to the side there and let us by."

I thought he was going to kill Lee. "No!" I hollered, and lifted my lance and flung it straight at the shotgunner's face. Startled by my yell, he half-turned toward me, jerking up his arms and the shotgun to shield himself. At the same time Lee, moving quicker than I could clearly see, slipped from his horse, lunged forward, grabbed the shotgun and twisted it from the man's hands. He backed off a couple of steps, watching the men closely, the shotgun at the ready.

"You don't point these things at people," Lee said, breathing a little faster than normal. His horse, alarmed by the scuffle, had spooked and was clattering around on the rocks, dragging the reins. "Get my horse, Billy."

I didn't want to miss anything; I stayed where I was.

"Now," Lee said, "you there in the back seat: pass that rifle this way. Butt first."

The man in back had raised the rifle so that it now pointed at the sky; he still held the bottle in his left hand. Eyes fixed on Lee, he fumbled around for a steady place to set the bottle down. "Hold this bottle," he said, groping with it toward the driver, keeping his eyes on Lee.

"Keep the bottle," Lee said; he leveled the shotgun so that it covered all three men. "Just pass me the rifle."

"Can't you see he's crazy?" the driver said; "give him the gun."

The man in the rear hesitated, glaring at Lee, ugly hatred on his face. "Is that shotgun loaded?" he growled to the man in front.

"My God yes it's loaded. Give him the rifle."

"I ought to kill him."

"For godsake give him the rifle."

The man on the back seat hesitated again. "I ought to kill him," he said, before sliding the rifle, buttplate first, over the shoulder of the man in the middle and toward Lee. The middle man relayed the rifle to Lee, who reached forward carefully with his left hand, accepted the weapon, and backed up again.

"Now to get back to the subject," he said, setting down the rifle but keeping the shotgun. "Did you see our horse?"

"We didn't see any horse," the driver mumbled.

Lee stared at him. "You're probably lying."

"We didn't see your horse."

Lee was silent for a little while. "All right," he said. "You fellas can go on home now."

"Give us our guns."

"I don't think I will," Lee said. "I don't think you people are big enough to play with these things. I ought to bust them over a rock, throw the pieces down the mountain." He paused. "But I'll do you a favor. I'll leave them at the Sheriff's office in Alamogordo. You can pick them up there. Now get out of here. There's something about you fellas that makes me very sick."

The driver began pumping the starter and gas pedal again.

"Wait a minute," Lee said. The driver stopped. "Get that coyote off the fender."

They gaped at him. "What?" the driver said.

"Leave the coyote here."

"Hold on," the man in back said. "That's my coyote. I killed him myself. He's mine."

"No, he belongs here." Lee pulled out his pocket-knife and opened it. Keeping the men covered with the shotgun, he stepped forward and cut the cord that bound the coyote to the fender and hood of the jeep. The body slid off, falling to the side of the road. "Now you can go," Lee said, moving back out of the way.

I moved too, turning Blue to the inside of the road, hard against the slope. Lee's horse had stopped a few yards farther down the road, watching the proceedings.

The driver of the jeep ground the starter and pumped on the gas pedal. The carburetor was still flooded.

"Let me give you some advice," Lee said. "Don't pump on the gas when you're flooded. That only makes it worse."

The driver scowled at him. "You shut up. I'll manage this thing without any help from you." He released the brake and the jeep started to roll forward, passing us.

"Goodbye," Lee shouted after them. "Drive carefully."

"Drive carefully," I echoed.

They rolled down the road without replying, without looking back, while the motor gasped and coughed, choking on gasoline. In a minute they were out of sight and gone. I rode after Lee's horse, caught it and brought it back to him. Lee sat on a rock, wiping the sweat from his face with a handkerchief and airing out his hat. "Thanks, Billy. My God it's hot."

My body was trembling. I felt too weak to get down off my horse.

"What a day," Lee said. He grinned up at me. "What happened, anyway?"

"I thought—I thought he was going to shoot you."

"And you threw that spear at him?" We looked at the yucca stalk, lying on the road near the body of the coyote. We looked at the coyote. "Now why did I do that?" Lee asked. He got up slowly, replacing his hat on his head, took the coyote by the scruff of the neck, hauled him to the edge of the road and let him roll down into the woods. After a moment he came back to his rock in the shade and sat down again.

"What about the guns?"

"Yeah, the guns." He looked at the guns. "We'll stash them here in the rocks and pick them up on the way home tomorrow." He sighed, a little wearily, then smiled at me. "Billy, would you mind getting that canteen out of the saddlebags? And I think you'll find something to eat in there too."

"You bet, Lee." Shakily, I got off my horse.

"Billy?"

"Yes?"

"You know, Billy, that was a foolish thing I did. I could've got both of us killed. But those—those men made me so goddamned angry. They had no manners at all."

"That's right," I said, unbuckling Lee's saddlebag. "No manners at all."

He sat musing, hat pushed back. "I wonder if they were officers or enlisted men?"

"They sure weren't gentlemen."

"I was an officer myself. That's why I find it hard to tell." He glanced at the tough sun blazing over us. "Well, anyway, I hope they make it down the mountain all right."

"I hope they don't."

"It's a good thing your grandfather wasn't here. He'd have killed those fellows. Strangled them with his bare hands." I handed Lee the canteen and a sandwich wrapped in waxed paper. "One other thing, Billy . . ."

"What?" I unwrapped a sandwich.

"Better not tell him about this."

"About the canteen?"

"About this incident here. The men in the jeep."

"Why not, Lee?"

"I'm afraid the old man might—do something drastic. Might go a little too far. We better not tell him, Billy."

"Okay, Lee, if you think that's best."

"I think it's best. We better not tell him." The horses, tied to the nearest pine, stamped their hooves as we prepared to eat. Lee looked at them. "You two be quiet. Don't you know there's a lion up here?"

The horses stared at Lee.

"That's right," he said. "A lion."

The horses stood perfectly quiet. Lee grinned at me. "Now we can eat."

We rested for an hour or so during the noon heat, then remounted and continued the climb up the mountainside. All afternoon we searched for the buckskin pony, following out the side trails, exploring the scrub oak thickets and the juniper jungles. When we reached the place where the old mine road joined our wagon road we checked that too, backtracking the jeep for several miles to the north, clear to the boundary of the White Sands Missile Range, a padlocked steel gate and a steel picket fence that stretched eastward, as far as the eye could follow, down through the hills and across the desert plain, and westward up the mountainside toward the pass between Thieves' Peak and the beginning of the San Andres chain of mountains. About eighty miles northwest of where we stood, admiring the DANGER—KEEP OUT signs, lay the site of the first atomic bomb explosion.

Returning from there, we followed wandering deer paths and cattle trails along the spine of a ridge that led toward a junction of two other ridges high on the east side of Thieves' Mountain. Up in there, too far away to see, was the perennial spring, the corral, and the old log cabin where we would camp overnight. And far above the camp, above timberline, the naked and jagged peak soared into the blue.

"What's up there?" I pointed toward the summit.

"What do you see up there?" Lee's gaze followed my pointing finger.

"Well," I said, "I don't see anything up there."

Lee was silent. He lowered his head, returning his eyes to the trail and terrain ahead of us.

"There must be something up there," I insisted.

"What are you looking for?"

"I don't know," I said. "Something."

"You won't find it up there."

"How do you know, Lee? Were you up there?"

"Yes, I climbed it once. On foot. You can't get a horse all the way to the top."

"Well, you must have seen something up there." He did not answer. "What did you see up there, Lee?"

"Good God," he said. "I mean, my God, you're persistent." He smiled at me. "You really got the disease, don't you."

"What disease?"

"The disease. I don't know what else to call it, I already feel sorry for the woman who marries you."

"I'm not going to marry anybody. I like horses better."

"That's a twist."

"All right," I said patiently. "When you went up there, Lee, what did you find? I mean, besides rock?"

"Besides rock? Well—I found a little grass. Not much. A strange green kind of grass. And some tiny little flowers. Tiny flowers, no bigger than snowflakes." He paused. "Some wild-sheep droppings. One eagle's nest." He stopped.

"What else?"

"That's about it."

Lee fell silent again. We rode quietly side by side, through a glade among the stunted pine trees. The quick wild birds flew before us, the sky deep and silent over their spontaneous cries. I waited.

"Are you positive you were up there, Lee?"

"Look," he said, pointing to sharp hoofprints intersecting the trail ahead of us. "A buck and a couple of does *pase por aqui* not five minutes ago. See where one of them peed on the ground? Not five minutes ago. We should've seen them. I must be getting old."

"How old are you, Lee,"

"Last year I was thirty-three. Old enough to be crucified. I got married instead. Next year I'll be thirty-five. Old enough to run for President."

"Are you going to run for President?"

"I'd rather be right than be wrong. My country, right or wrong? There's talk about it, Billy. There's a ground swell of support appearing in Guadalupe County. The grass roots are growing and I'm mending my fences."

"Let's talk about something important."

"Like what? What could that be?"

"I'm hungry."

"You can say that again."

"I'm hungry."

"Now you're talking. Now you're making sense. Let's jog up these here saddleracks and see what the old man has for supper."

The sun was hanging close to the shoulder of the mountain, roaring down from the cloudless sky, when Lee and I regained the old wagon road and measured its final few switchbacks up to the bench of level ground where the corral and cabin stood. We saw the sorrel stallion, barebacked and glossy, staked out in the little dry park in front of the corral. A thread of smoke dangled over the cabin chimney and Grandfather himself, when he heard our horses, appeared in the open doorway.

"Evening," he said. "I thought you boys would show about now. I got three cans of beans and a panful of corned beef warming up on the stove."

"That'll do for a start," Lee said.

We dismounted and unsaddled our horses. I was tired. In fact the saddle, as I lugged it to the corral fence, seemed to weigh approximately five hundred pounds.

"You can just turn old Blue loose, Billy," Grandfather said. "He'll stick close to Rocky. You might brush him down a little."

Lee picketed his horse. We curried our animals with juniper twigs and then went into the cabin, following the scent of food. The inside of the cabin was neat and clean, was furnished with an iron cot, a table and chairs, a cupboard full of canned goods, a kerosene lamp, and other supplies, including a sack of grain suspended on baling wire from the rafters to make life more difficult for the mice and squirrels. A pot of coffee simmered on the stove.

"That smells good," Lee said.

"Ain't quite ready yet," the old man said, stirring the corned beef with a fork. He handed me the empty water bucket. "Billy, would you mind filling that? We'll be ready to eat as soon as you get back."

"Yes sir." I swallowed my disappointment, took the bucket, left the cabin and walked along the footpath toward the spring at the head of the ravine. The path led downward along the base of a cliff, winding among boulders big as boxcars and under tall stately yellow pines, until it reached a sort of glen or grotto in a deep fold of the mountainside. The air felt cool, the light was green and filtered down in there—I thought of the lion. I knelt by the sandy basin of the spring and drank from my cupped hands before filling the pail. The glen was very quiet; I could hear no breeze, no bird cries, no sound at all except the gentle purr of the water as it glided over moss-covered rocks and sank out of sight into the mud and weeds below the spring.

I returned to the cabin, the bucket of water pulling down my arm and shoulder. Grandfather was dishing out the food into tin plates and pouring the coffee. Lee stood near the corral, feeding grain to the horses.

"Come and get it!" Grandfather shouted. To me he

said, "Put the water on the stove, Billy, and bring your plate outside. Too hot to eat in here."

The three of us sat on the grass against the cabin wall, in the shade, and faced the sunlit world below. We were all silent for a while and too busy to admire the spectacular view, eating what I thought was probably the best meal I had ever had in my life. Later, after second helpings all around, full and comforted, we set our plates aside and began to talk and look at things again.

"How could I forget my cigars."

"Have a tailormade," Lee said, offering a cigarette to the old man.

Grandfather examined the cigarette. "They say women enjoy these things."

"That's right," Lee said, "and I enjoy women." He offered his pack to me. "Cigarette, Billy?"

I hesitated. I wasn't allowed to smoke, of course. Besides, I preferred the corncob pipe I had hidden in my suitcase back at the ranch-house.

"Put them back," Grandfather said. "Don't give the boy one of those."

"Why not?"

"It's a filthy, evil, despicable habit, a disgrace to the human race." Grandfather lit his cigarette and took a deep drag. "He's too young. Put them back."

They smoked. I pulled a stem of grass and chewed on it and looked. There was much to look at from where we sat. With the great mountain at our backs, we had a full and open view to the north, east and south—one-half the known world. I could see four different mountain systems, not counting the one holding me up, the lights of two cities, and about seven thousand square miles of the desert in between. I saw the San Andres Mountains rolling north, the Sacramento Mountains beyond Alamogordo, forty miles away to the northeast, the Guadalupe Mountains some eighty miles due east and the Oregon Mountains and the hazy smudge of El Paso far to the south, with the deserts of Chihuahua spreading toward infinity beyond.

The sun dropped lower. I saw the shadow of Thieves' Peak creep across the plain toward Grandfather Vogelin's ranch, toward the village of Baker, toward the Guadalupe Mountains, reaching out to meet the curtain of darkness coming toward us from the east.

"Grandfather?"

"Yes?"

"Did you ever climb the mountain?"

"What mountain?"

"The one above us. Thieves' Mountain."

"No, can't say I did. And I never will. This cabin here's high enough for me. About as close to Heaven as I ever want to get. You can bury me here."

"We'll need dynamite for that," Lee said.

"Here Lies John Vogelin: Born Forty Years Too Late, Died Forty Years Too Soon," Grandfather said.

"Why forty years too soon?"

"I figure in forty years civilization will collapse and everything will be back to normal. I wish I could live to see it."

"Why? You'd be right back were you started from."

"I'd like that. That's the place to end up."

"Don't you want to get ahead?" Lee grinned at me.

"I'd rather stay behind. I already got a head."

"You already got a behind, where your head ought to be."

"Don't confuse me. It took me seventy years to figure this much out. Who's going to water the horses?"

Nobody spoke. I stared out at the approaching union of light and dark. Lee and Grandfather stared at me.

"Okay," Grandfather said, "we'll try again: who's going to wash the dishes?"

"I'll water the horses," I said.

"Fine. If you start right away you'll still have time to wash the dishes."

"I'll light the lamp for you," Lee said, "when you're

through watering the horses. So you don't have to wash the dishes in the dark."

"Thanks," I said. "But us real cowboys always wash our dishes in the sand."

Lee was silent.

"Lee, you lose," Grandfather said. "You wash the dishes. The boy's whipped you again. Billy, you'll find another old bucket inside the corral."

"Why can't I just take the horses down to the spring?"

"That boy asks a lot of questions," Lee said.

They stared at me hopefully.

"All right," I said, "why not? That's all I asked. Wouldn't it be easier to take the horses to the spring than to carry the spring back here to the horses?"

"A bucket is lighter than a horse," Lee pointed out.

"The horses can *walk*," I said.

"But they're tired."

"Will you please answer my question?"

The old man smiled and patted my knee. "You're right, Billy, it should be easier to do it your way. But the horses don't like it down in there. And the trail is too tight for all three at once; you'd have a rough time. And besides, think what a mess three big horses, full of water and grass and grain, would make of one little spring which is barely big enough to dip a pail into. We drink out of that spring too."

"I guess you're right, Grandfather. I should've thought of that." I stood up.

"Someday we'll cover the spring, run a pipe from it down to a water trough the horses can get to."

"How long have you been using this place?" Lee asked, winking at me. "How many years, John?"

"You shut up and wash your dishes."

I walked to the corral, found the bucket and started down the path to the spring. Lee and the old man rose to their feet, stretching. "We'll give you a hand, Billy," Grandfather said, "as soon as we clean up."

"Yes sir."

The twilight was moving in. I had to go carefully to find my way, for the trail seemed awfully vague in the deep shadows under the cliff. When I reached the spring the tree toads were bleating, a dismal noise and a sure sign of night. There was no other sound, except the murmur of the flowing water. A few fireflies twinkled in the gloom above the weeds.

The long day in the desert sun had drawn a lot of water from my body. I was thirsty again. I squatted close to the spring, scooped up a double handful of water and drank. I dipped up more and bathed my face.

When the last tinkle of falling drops had died away I became aware of a deep and unexpected silence. The toads had gone silent and the water seemed to run more quietly than before. Even the fireflies had disappeared. I waited for a moment, listening to the silence, then reached cautiously for the bucket and dipped it into the water as quietly as I could, afraid to make too much noise. Looking around in all directions I could see nothing, nothing but the damp weeds, the wall of rock, the grand trunks of the yellow pines, the dusky woods. I looked up.

I should not have looked up. On the brink of the crag above the spring I saw a pair of yellow eyes gleaming in a sleek head, saw a dark powerful shape of unforeseeable hugeness crouched as if to leap. I could not move, I could not make a sound. I stared up at the lion and the lion stared down at me. Paralyzed, I squatted by the spring, gripping the water bucket and unconscious of the ache in my muscles, and waited for death to fall upon me.

My grandfather called through the silence, from the far-away cabin out of sight and out of reach beyond the twilight: "Billy?"

I tried to answer but my throat was numb. The lion watched me.

My grandfather called again: "Billy? Where are you?"

This time the lion turned his massive head and with

his yellow eyes looked blandly, without curiosity or fear, up the pathway.

I heard the old man's boots scraping on the stones of the path, coming toward me, and at last the big cat stirred himself and rose and vanished, all at once, suddenly, with uncanny grace and stillness, into the night and the forest.

Grandfather called me for the third time, coming closer, and now I thought I could answer. "Here," I croaked. "I'm here." I managed to stand up, the heavy bucket frozen in my grip. As the old man came toward me down the path I took a few leaden steps to meet him.

He stared at my face. "What happened to you?"

I told him.

He put one arm around my shaking shoulders and with his other hand unwrapped my fingers one by one from the handle of the water bucket. Carrying the water himself, he led me up the pathway among the boulders to the cabin where Lee waited for us in the welcome glow of the lamp.

"What's wrong?" Lee said, wiping a tin plate with a bandana.

"He saw it."

"Saw what?"

"The lion."

"Ah. . . ." said Lee. He looked at me and smiled, his deep eyes tender. "You're a lucky boy." He gripped my arm. "How about a cup of your grampaw's coffee?"

"Yes," I said calmly. "I can drink anything."

A little later all three of us went back to the spring, with both buckets, and looked around. Lee even climbed up to the ledge above the spring but by that time it was too dark to see any tracks. We went back up the trail, watered the horses, built a little squaw fire outside between the cabin and the corral, and unrolled the sleeping bags which the old man kept in the cabin. We sat around the fire for a while after that, watching the moon over the eastern ranges, and talked of the

lion, the lost horse, the next day's work, in which Lee
announced he would not be able to join—he was leaving us in the morning. But he promised to come back
to the ranch in two or three days.

"What does a mountain lion sound like?" I asked.

"Well," Grandfather, "like a woman. Like a woman
screaming. How would you describe it, Lee?"

Lee considered. *"Compadres,* a lion does sound
something like a woman. Like a vampire-woman wail-
ing for her demon lover."

"Are we going to hunt the lion, Grandfather?"

"No, we'll let well enough alone. If we don't hunt
him, why he won't hurt us. Besides, it's the only lion
left on the place. I can't afford to lose him."

"Do you think he's watching us now?"

"I wouldn't be surprised."

Nobody said anything for a minute or so. The moon
crept up into the stars. I added more sticks to the fire.

Grandfather stretched his arms and yawned. "I don't
know about you men but I am tired. Anybody want to
sleep on the cot inside?"

Lee grinned. "Is there room for all three of us?"

"Not with me in the middle there ain't."

"Then let's all sleep out here."

"By the fire," I said.

"You boys do that," Grandfather said, "but somebody might as well use that cot. I've been sleeping on
the ground for about seventy years now, give or take
a few."

"You ought to be used to it," Lee said.

"I'm used to it. But I never did like it much." Picking up his bedroll, the old man walked toward the cabin
door. "Goodnight, gentlemen."

"Goodnight," we said.

Lee and I shook the scorpions and black widow
spiders out of the sleeping bags, spread them out again
on the ground close to the fire, removed our boots and
hats and crawled inside. We did not use our saddles for
pillows. A saddle is hard enough just to sit on.

At first I lay on my side, gazing at the coals of the burning pine. Then I lay on my back and stared straight up at the marvelous stars. The flaming blue stars. Out in the little park the horses stumbled around, munching grass, and I heard one of them staling on the hard ground. A meteor stroked quietly halfway across the sky.

"Lee?"

"Yes?"

"Up there on the peak: Was it—something like the lion?"

He did not answer at once. "Would you mind repeating that question?"

"What you found up there—was it something like the lion?"

"Oh. Yes. Yes, Billy. It was something like the lion."

I thought about that as I looked straight up at the stars. The marvelous stars. A marvelous day. The stars became dimmer as I watched them, as if they were drifting farther and farther away from us. I closed my eyes and slept and dreamed of the missing pony, fireflies, a pair of yellow eyes.

Billy!

I opened my eyes. Dark.

Wake up, Billy.

I poked my head out of the sleeping bag and for a moment thought I had not slept at all. Then I saw the blue streaks of dawn and the ashes of the fire. I looked toward the cabin and saw the old man already at work by lamplight, serving breakfast at the table inside the open door. I smelled coffee and bacon. He looked out and called me again: "Out of the sack! Let's eat!"

I struggled out into the chill mountain morning. Shivering, I pulled the cold stiff boots onto my feet, found my hat, and stood up. Lee was bringing in the horses. Blinking, rubbing my face, I hobbled toward him and helped tie all three near the cabin. My legs and back were so stiff and sore I thought the horses must have spent part of the night tramping on me to keep warm.

"How do you feel today, Billy?" Lee Mackie grinned at me in the morning dusk; all those white teeth—no wonder he thought people would vote for him.

"I feel pretty good," I said. "Pretty damn good."

He laughed and slapped my back. "Come on, let's eat."

The old man was banging on the skillet with a big spoon. "Get in here!" he hollered, "or I'll throw it to the bluejays."

After breakfast we grained the horses and saddled up. Again somebody had to go after water: I volunteered. Wanted to prove something. I made two trips down to the spring, and the second time climbed the rocks to the place where the lion had been crouching. I could not see any tracks but thought I detected a strange odor in the air—a feline smell. No, something else: ozone and summer lightning.

We closed up the cabin, climbed on our horses and moved out, starting down the ancient trail road toward the foothills. Grandfather and I planned to explore the territory between the mine road and the windmill. Lee would ride with us as far as the junction of the two roads.

My bones felt like cast iron, my rear like one unanimous saddle sore, but once astride the bulk and power and restless life of Blue I didn't care. The feel of the reins in my hand, the creak and squeak of leather, the big horse beneath me, gave me all the strength and confidence I needed. I felt like a lion: an aged, battered but still mighty lion. With joy in my heart and satisfaction in my mind I rode beside my friends and watched the shoals of green and yellow clouds spread out like burning islands on the sea of the eastern sky.

"We'll have rain today," Grandfather said, squinting at the sky through his wise steel-rimmed spectacles. "Not much, naturally, just a thundershower. About one sixty-fourth of an inch of water and all the thunder and lightning we need."

"When?" Lee asked.

"Oh, about one-thirty. Make it one forty-five."

"I'm going to check that prophecy with the Weather Bureau. If you're wrong it'll cost you one gallon of Bacardi. In a wickerwork basket."

"You've got yourself a bet, young fella. Shake."

They shook hands.

The nighthawks soared and plunged against the light, aware of the imminent sun. A raven croaked like a witch from a dead pine down below, reminding the nighthawks that their time was almost up. Magpies appeared, hungry birds in academic black and white, who squawked and squawled like quarreling theologians as they gathered. A canyon wren woke up, singing her trickling-water song.

"Is Heaven better than this place?" I asked.

"The climate's a little better here," Grandfather answered.

"Less humility," Lee said.

Three long switchbacks down through the woods brought us to the joining of the roads and the separation of our little band.

"I'm sorry I can't stick with you today," Lee said to Grandfather and me. "But I wish you luck; I hope you find that invisible horse."

"I have a hunch that horse would be better off if he was invisible," the old man said, scanning the ridges north and east.

"You'll find him," Lee said. "Anyway, I'll see you both in a couple of days."

"Bring Annie along next time."

"I'll try. I'll try to do that." Smiling, he gave us a salute, turned his horse and rode down the trail, through the high hairy weeds and whiskery flowers thriving among the rocks and faded ruts of the road.

I was sorry to see him ride away. Most of the magic I had felt during this expedition seemed to float away with him. I thought of our glorious victory on the day before and wondered if we'd ever have another like it. Certainly not today. Lee Mackie gave us a final wave and disappeared around the first bend below.

"Let's go, Billy."

I rode beside my grandfather over the same road Lee and I had taken. The old man apparently shared my mood. He was silent for a long time as we pushed our horses north.

"I see we had a jeep in here not too long ago," he finally said. "On a one-way trip. I know how they came in; I wonder how they went out."

I didn't say anything.

"I hope they found their way out all right. I mean, without coming across any of our livestock. Our gun-happy friends from the other side of the wire seem to have trouble, sometimes, in distinguishing a beef cow from a wild jack rabbit."

"Yes," I said.

He looked at me. "You feel all right, Billy?"

"Yes sir. I feel fine."

"You're not tired, are you? I realize you had a rough day yesterday, all that mileage on a horse after nine months on your—at your schoolwork."

"Honest, Grandfather, I feel fine." I sat up straighter and looked at things sharply, taking an interest. And almost at once I did feel better again.

"That's good. We have a lot of ground to cover today."

We covered a lot of ground. We left the old mine road and picked our way through the brush and cactus of the hills below it, following cattle trails, deer paths and no paths at all. It was hot, sweaty work, with the sun and humidity rising, the dust getting in my teeth and eyes, the juniper branches whipping in my face. All morning we scouted the hills and searched the canyons, working our way gradually downward until, close to noon, we came out on the desert not far from the gathering pen, the windmill and the big tank full of all that cool green water. Nothing ever smelled better to me as our tired brutes trotted toward it, picking up their pace. Nothing ever tasted sweeter. Faces dripping, the old man and I smiled at each other and dipped our heads for more. Rocky and Blue did the same and the flies buzzed happily over us all.

Afterwards we rested in the latticed, inadequate shade of the windmill, chewing on the jerky which the old man brought from his saddlebags. The air was hot and still, the windmill static, though far off in the desert we could see the play of the whirlwinds, pillars of dust dancing like ghosts over the plain.

While the dust-devils played on the lowlands the clouds were piling up on the crest of the mountains, great cumuli-nimbi charged with lightning and thunder, dark with power and possible rain.

The clouds formed, the whirlwinds danced, but the air of the desert remained static as a sea of glass, full of heat and suspense, but inert. Inert—like us. We did not talk. I gazed at the sky and the clouds, and the old man, stretched on the ground with his hat over his face, snored softly in his slumber. I wanted to sleep myself but I couldn't—a strange excitement kept my nerves alert, and I felt the rapid beating of my heart.

Nothing would happen today. The sun would fall over the mountains, the clouds grumble and the buzzards soar, but nothing would happen. I knew that. And to me it seemed all so marvelous I liked it that way. I wanted no irrelevant event to mar or cut short the crystal stasis of the long deep desert afternoon. Tonight, perhaps. Or tomorrow. But not this day.

The clouds spoke in a muted rumble over the barren mountains and a flicker of lightning, like an illuminated nerve, shot through the tallest of the thunderheads. The roll of thunder faded off and nothing happened.

I rolled over and lay on my belly, pulled a stem of timothy from its casing, chewed on it and stared at the flies and ants and beetles crawling sluggishly about in the shady weeds at the base of the water tank. A slender straw-colored scorpion emerged from a crevice beneath a stone, crawling toward a fly. The fly, unaware, was inspecting a fragment of cow dung with his nervous forelegs. The scorpion glided close, the tail with its poison bulb and red curved stinger arched above the head, the big crab claws reaching forward. The fly took off. I killed the scorpion. Not because he was a scorpion but because he was unlucky.

The old man grunted, pushed back his hat and opened his red-rimmed eyes. He squinted at the sun, high in the western sky, and stood up. I heard the creak of his old joints. "Mount up, Billy. We'll take one more look for that buckskin."

Blue stood with drooping neck and closed eyes in the same poor shade of the windmill, shaking his head, twitching his skin, brushing his tail at the idle flies. I saddled him and climbed aboard. With some reluctance the big horse allowed me to guide him after Grandfather, headed not for home but for the hills again.

We took a different trail this time, one farther to the north and not so steep, that led toward the pass between Thieves' Mountain and the San Andres. As we slowly climbed I was able to see more and more of the White Sands, that sea of milky dunes that stretched for fifty miles north and south between the desert ranges. Lost somewhere in the middle of that vastness were the new installations of the Proving Grounds.

Giant yuccas loomed up in silhouette before the wild sky and the piled-up masses of clouds. We passed a dead pinyon pine, lightning-blasted, stripped of all its bark, the nude limbs gleaming like silver.

Three ravens flopped off and lumbered away at our approach, squawking like housewives, alarming the pinyon jays higher on the hillside, who at once set up an answering clamor of their own which sounded like "Rain! rain! rain!"

The thunderheads were closer now, as the trail led up toward the mountains. I saw another scribble of lightning pass through the chasms of the clouds and after a long pause heard the barrage of thunder. But the sun rode clear, the vibrant light blazed down. Higher and higher we rode until we reached the crest of a long ridge and the pinyon-juniper belt once more. Here the air was a few degrees cooler and I felt for the first time the stirring of the troubled air over the mountains.

The old man shouted: "Over there!" He pointed toward the slope of the adjacent ridge, half a mile north. "There he is!" I looked hard but saw nothing alive, saw nothing move except a flight of black wings circling in the sky. My grandfather drew up his horse and waited for me. I stopped near him on the narrow trail and followed with my eyes the line of his arm and forefinger. "You see him, Billy?"

I scrutinized the hillside, the tangle of mesquite, yucca and oak brush, the jumbled boulders dappled with cloud shadows. "No sir."

"Halfway up the hill. See that yellow outcrop,"

I stared closely.

"Just to the left and a little above it. There's old Rascal."

Then I saw it, the yellowish shape of a horse spread motionless on the ground. "He's down, Grandfather."

"He should be. He's dead. Can't you see, his belly's torn open. Look, the birds are on him now."

I saw the black buzzards crawling like flies over the prone figure and saw three more buzzards descend. "What happened to him?"

"Let's find out." Grandfather spurred Rocky forward. We rode further up the trail till we reached a point on a level with the dead horse, left the trail and made our way through juniper and chaparral around the head of the canyon to the farther ridge. We could no longer see Rascal but we were guided by the scavengers as they circled over him.

We picked our way through the jungle of brush and rock, inventing a trail, until we came within sight and smell of our object. The stench was bad and the horse hardly recognizable as the one I'd known so well and ridden so much the summer before.

We rode close; the vultures ascended in a cloud of black wings, rags of rotten flesh hanging from their beaks, and circled above the trees.

The horse lay on his side, completely disembowled, the entrails strewn over the stones, the neck and flank ripped open, the eye sockets empty. The smell was so foul we had to ride around him and approach again from the upwind side. Grandfather studied the ground. "The lion was here," he said. On a patch of dust he showed me the broad round print of the lion's paw.

"Maybe the lion killed him, Grandfather."

"I don't think it likely." The old man dismounted, letting his horse stand with dangling reins, and walked up to the carcass. I stayed where I was, ten feet away. For several minutes Grandfather stared down at the ruin of our horse. "Have a look at this, Billy." He motioned to me to come closer.

"I don't feel very good."

"You feel sick?"

"Yes sir."

He nodded, stayed a minute longer, then came back to his horse, stumbling a little on his high heels over the loose rock. He mounted, adjusted his hat, turned the horse and started back the way we had come. I had a glimpse of the dull bewildered fury in his eyes before he turned his back to me.

Afraid to ask any questions, I followed in silence. We reached the trail and proceeded downhill toward home, the horses stepping a bit livelier now. Overhead the clouds boiled and thickened, obscuring the sun, and the thunder boomed louder and louder. I shivered, knotted my bandana around my neck and turned up my collar. Raindrops fell on the warm boulders beside the trail, spattering the stone with dark spots of moisture which faded as I watched and evaporated into nothing.

We rode at a fast walk down the trail, followed

closely by the forward fringe of the storm. Lightning barked in our rear, casting white flashes of light over the shaking boughs of the pinyons and junipers around us. When I saw Grandfather untie the poncho packed behind the cantle of his saddle I knew we were in for it and I untied mine too. Lightning struck again, so close that I cringed, and old Blue danced forward like a colt. We let our horses break into a trot. I stood up in the stirrups and supported myself with one hand on the saddlehorn. All the aches and pains I'd felt in the morning came back to me now with redoubled emphasis. I wished there weren't so many miles still remaining between us and the ranch-house.

I looked up. The sky was no longer in sight: instead of a sky we had a low ceiling of cloudmass, purple, swollen and turbulent. Far to the east, however, the sky was still clear and the desert below glowed in the sunlight.

Another flurry of rain fell around us and this time the drops did not fade but multiplied and merged with one another until the surface of the rock gleamed with a uniform wetness. At the same time I realized my shirt was getting wet: I put on the rubber poncho.

We reached the foot of the trail, trotted past the windmill and corral and headed east on the dirt road home. The golden plains extended before us clear to the Guadalupes, shining with light, but the edge of that light receded faster than our advance and a moment later the clouds burst open overhead and down it came, the deluge.

Cold rain pelted my back and shoulders and a continuous stream of water poured off the forward brim of my hat onto Blue's neck. The road softened beneath us, sand and earth changing into mud, and the horses' hooves made a spongy sound. My new straw hat began to wilt as the water soaked through it into my hair. Water ran in icy strings down my neck and inside my shirt. I felt miserable—wet, cold, tired, hungry. I found myself hating the bellow of thunder, the lightning with its dazzling glare on the soaked shrubs and darkened earth around us.

But five minutes later, abruptly, the rain stopped, the lightning ceased and the thunder rolled back to the mountaintops in a series of echoing reverberations from Thieves' Mountain to the San Andres.

The sun reappeared, burning through a gulf in the shrunken clouds, and blazed on our steaming backs. I took off the poncho and hung my soggy hat on the horn, reshaping it more to my fancy while it was in a malleable condition.

We were nearly home. A mile ahead we could see the cottonwoods along the Salado, the group of ranch buildings, and the red *barrancas* beyond. Every detail of the landscape stood out clearly in the slanting amber evening light: I saw the ravens in the trees, Grandfather's pickup truck parked in the wagonshed, the ranch-house windows aflame with the sun, the Peralta children playing by the windmill, the dogs shaking themselves on the porch, the folds and creases of the eroded clay banks on the far side of the buildings, the chamisa and greasewood glistening on the plain— things, appearances, surfaces vividly precise, dogmatically real, and all of it surmounted by a triumphal double rainbow.

I thought I heard the roll of thunder again. Riding beside Grandfather, I saw him peering to the north, toward the upper reaches of the Salado River. The sound of thunder became continuous, a steady distant roar. "We better hurry," he said, "the flood's coming." Our horses had slowed to a walk when the rain stopped; now we jogged them up again and trotted toward the wash.

As we rode through the grove of cottonwoods under the leaves already dry and fluttering, we heard the roar of the approaching flood come round the bend, though the water itself was still out of sight. The sound now was like that of a railway train.

We splashed through the stream of clear water and

trotted over the sand, the riverbed dry and hot and bright under a clean sky. But before we reached the far side the forelip of the flash flood came rolling around the upstream turn and surged toward us.

Inevitably surprised, I drew up Blue and stopped to watch. The horse fought the bit, stepping sideways. Grandfather turned. "Get outa there!" he shouted. "What's the matter with you?" Unwillingly at first I gave in, letting the horse start ahead and lope on across the riverbed and up the bank to safety. There I stopped him again and watched the approach of the flood.

Red-brown and thick with mud, splattered with scum and lacy jags of foam, tossing a broken tree on its crest, the flood poured like gravy down the sunny wash. The front of it advanced on a curve in a wall about a foot high, moving as fast as a tired man could run, and swirling out toward each side. Rainbows glittered in the spray, white-caps formed and disappeared and re-formed on the roiling surface as the flood came down in greater strength, deepening, shaking the ground on which we stood, filling our ears with its tremendous rumble.

"There goes New Mexico," the old man shouted at me from a few feet away. "Down the river!" He watched for only a moment, his face somber, then rode away. I stayed for a while, though old Blue stamped and yawed beneath me, in a hurry to get to the corral. Finally I let him have his way: we were both hungry.

By the time I got the horses unsaddled and brushed and at their feed the sun was down. My legs felt hollow, my knees trembled like a baby's, as I walked toward the ranch-house and the wonderful smell of supper. It was easy to forget the dead horse back in the hills, my pony Rascal rotting away in the soft twilight while the birds sang around him, and the red ants, the beetles and blowflies, attacked his poor stinking corpse.

3

"No!" Grandfather shouted. "Shot, I tell you! His jaw smashed. Didn't kill him right away either—the poor brute must have lived for hours. Trying to get back here. They shot him, by God! With a hollow-point bullet, looked like. A hole big as my fist where the slug came out." The old man slammed his fist on the kitchen table and the lamp jumped and the light and shadows swam crazily over the walls.

Lee studied his cigarette. I worked on my letter home —I'd written one paragraph and didn't know what else to say, without lying too much. Since there was nothing more I wanted to write I sketched a picture of myself on horseback riding across the White Sands with two buzzards circling above me and a black sun circling above the buzzards. I wasn't much interested in what I was doing. I was listening closely to the old man's anger and Lee Mackie's careful silences.

"Are they trying to *scare* me out of here?" Grandfather asked, chomping on his burnt-out cigar. "Are they fools enough to think they can *scare* me outa my ranch and my home?"

Lee spoke carefully. "Don't gallop off in all directions, John. You're the one that's talking foolish now. How do you know who shot the horse? Or why? Maybe it was an accident."

Some accident, I said to myself; we should've murdered those guys. . . .

"Too many accidents around here," the old man roared. "I suppose it's an accident when they drive trucks through my fences. I suppose it's just an accident their skyrockets come down on my range and scare the cows so bad we still ain't found them all. Poor old Eloy went all over the northwest sections today and couldn't find them creatures nowhere."

"They sound like accidents to me," Lee said. "Things like that have happened to other people around here. Besides, the military isn't run by hoodlums. They don't want enemies here—they want to make friends and influence people. Has DeSalius been here to see you yet?"

Grandfather tilted the rum jug in its wickerwork basket and refilled his glass, adding ice. He refilled Lee's glass and added ice. "DeSalius," he grumbled. "Who's DeSalius?"

"Colonel Everett Stone DeSalius, Corps of Engineers. Handles real estate matters for the Defense Department." Lee squeezed a little lime juice into his drink and dropped the rind into the glass.

I became aware of the patter of wings against the windowpane. One thousand millers were trying to get in, hungry for the light.

"This man DeSalius," Lee went on, "why you'll like him. You'll like him, John. You'll enjoy meeting him. Wears civvies and always carries a briefcase. Really a lawyer, not an engineer. Much less a soldier."

"I'll stuff his briefcase down his throat if he comes meddling around here," Grandfather said. "The Box V is not for sale. Yes sir, I'll stuff it down his throat and pound sand after it."

"He'll be around. You'll like him. And by the way he's holding a little secret meeting tonight in the county courthouse. You're invited of course. He's going to explain to Haggard and Reese and Vogelin and such diehards why it's their patriotic duty to sell their holdings for half what they're worth."

"Vogelin won't be there. I know about the meeting, they sent me a letter." Grandfather removed the cigar from his mouth and took a stiff drink. "I ain't going to be there."

"Be sensible, John."

"Sensible? Is that what you call sensible? Listen, I won't give an inch to those—scum. I will not give them any kind of satisfaction a-tall, damn them."

"You ought to come."

"Not a chance."

"I'm going. Do you want me to speak for you?"

"Go ahead if you want to waste your time. Tell them what I tell you: The Box V is not for sale and never will be for sale. Why, my father built this—"

"Built this house with his bare hands. Yeah, I know. And with the help of half a dozen Mexicans for wages of a dollar a day. Listen, John, you're beating your head against a stone wall. You got any sense you better deal with these people while they're in a friendly mood. If you make them condemn the land you might not get half of what they're offering now."

"I don't care about that. I don't want their dirty Government money. All I want is for them to let me alone, to let me work my ranch in peace, to let me die here and pass it on to my heir."

"Your heir?"

"My heir."

Lee hesitated. "What heir, John? Isabel's in Phoenix, Marian's in Albuquerque, Julie's in Pittsburgh. All happily married, so far as I can judge, all with children. You know none of them would ever come back to this God-forsook baked-out over-grazed non-profit-making parcel of dust and cactus. You're fooling yourself again. What heir?"

Grandfather stared at the glass in his hand, scowling. "I'll find an heir. You let me worry about that. And don't call this ranch over-grazed. I don't like that kind of talk."

"Of course you don't. But it's the truth."

Grandfather was silent for a moment. "It's the dry

spell," he said at last. "The drouth. It'll break pretty soon."

"This what you call a dry spell has lasted thirty years now."

"All the more reason to think it can't last much longer."

Lee smiled, sighed, and rubbed his eyes. "Old horse, you remind me of a hound dog I had once. He sat down on some prickly pear one day and right off began to howl. But would he get up? He would not. He was too stubborn to move. He knew his rights."

The old man squinted at Lee. "Sometimes you make me wonder just whose side you're on, Mackie."

Lee answered at once. "I'm on your side, John, and you know it. That's why I'm trying to talk some sense into your head. I want to see you make the best of a sorry proposition. I don't want you to get into a lot of trouble and maybe lose all you have for nothing."

"I'm not going to lose it. I'm going to keep it. Even if I have to fight for it all over again, like my father did back in the seventies. Now tell me: Whose side are you on?"

"If you decide to fight I'll fight for you. You don't have to ask me that. But I hope you change your feeble old mind before we both end up in Leavenworth."

Grandfather smiled: his gold tooth gleamed in the lamplight. "That's all I wanted to hear, Lee."

"You've heard it before."

The old man turned to me. "Billy, you better finish that letter and get to bed. We have work to do tomorrow."

"Yes sir." I bent over my letter, licked the pen, and compelled myself to write a few more lines: *The weather is hot. Somebody shot Rascal. This summer I'm riding Blue. . . .* I felt Lee watching me, felt his friendly grin. There was a power in his steady level gaze that always strengthened me, that filled me, for a short while at least, with a shy, subtle but confident sense of happiness.

"Let the kid stay up a little longer. He promised to teach me how to play chess tonight. Didn't you, Billy?"

"Yes sir," I said.

"Thought you said you were going to that meeting," Grandfather said.

"Yeah, I know." Lee looked at his wristwatch: the silver band flashed on his brown forearm. "Well, I got half an hour to get there. You better come with me, John."

"I'll come on Judgment Day."

"That'll be any day now."

"Let it come. I'm ready."

Lee grinned, shrugged and pushed back his chair. Lazily he stood up and put on his hat. He stopped smiling and looked sternly at the old man. "Vogelin— you're a jackass."

"You might be right."

"You're heading straight for trouble—and heartbreak."

"We'll see."

"You're being downright irresponsible."

"That's a new one. Tell me about that."

"Next time." Lee turned to me, smiling. "Goodnight, Billy. Next time we'll get out your chess set. I won't ask you to try to talk any sense into your grandfather because I know you're just as stubborn and ignorant as he is."

"Yes sir," I said.

Colonel Everett Stone DeSalius appeared two days later, driving a gray government car with decals on the door that said United States Corps of Engineers. Grandfather, Eloy and I found him waiting for us when we came back from riding fence. Eloy and I took care of the horses. Grandfather went up to the house to meet our visitor, who was sitting on the porch steps. I hurried to join them, letting Eloy finish the work.

Colonel DeSalius was wearing civilian clothes, as Lee had promised—a trim summer suit of gray dacron, straw hat with narrow brim, white shirt with a silver-blue neck-tie. He was a big man, heavier than Grandfather, with a broad chest like a bull's and a powerful red neck. His blue eyes shone pleasantly, matching the necktie, and his complexion was bright and shiny: the man ate well. His smile, when he smiled, which was frequently, made you feel that this stranger was really an old friend of the family. I would have liked him except that he smiled too much.

He stood up when he saw Grandfather approaching and walked to meet him, extending his right hand. Reluctantly Grandfather shook hands with him and then invited the colonel to have a chair on the verandah. They sat down. The old man offered DeSalius a cigar, which he accepted with obvious pleasure. Since the day was hot—all days were hot that summer—Cruzita brought out ice water.

I arrived in time to hear the beginning of the conversation.

"Well, sir," the colonel said, "I suppose you know why I'm here."

"No," the old man said. "No, I don't."

The colonel opened his fat briefcase, drew out a paper and gave it to Grandfather. "Thought I'd deliver this to you personally, Mr. Vogelin. It's a notice of Declaration of Taking, with an order of immediate entry from the U.S. District Court, Judge Fagergren presiding, attached. Don't mind the harsh language, it's not as bad as it sounds. Let me try to explain: the Secretary of Defense, acting under authority of the Act of 1888, has filed in the U.S. District Court at Albuquerque a Declaration of Taking which subjects your fee-simple title to condemnation. I refer you to Volume Forty, U.S.C.A., Section two hundred and fifty. Now the Attorney General—"

"U.S.C.A.? What's that?"

"United States Code, Annotated. This filing of the Declaration of Taking in turn authorizes the Attorney General of the United States to proceed at once—see

Volume Forty again, U.S.C.A., Section two fifty-eight-
A—to proceed at once, following the *ex parte* hearing,
in taking possession of your property in behalf of the
Defense Department—formerly the War Department—
and opening it to immediate entry, because of the
urgency of the matter involved: national security."

DeSalius paused and took a deep breath, smiling at
the old man.

The old man spoke, slowly and distinctly: "My ranch
is not for sale."

"Yes." DeSalius rustled his documents and puffed
heartily on Grandfather's cigar. "Yes sir. We understand your feelings in this case. The negotiators have
reported your opposition to me already. It's because
you refused to sell or negotiate that we felt we had to
proceed with the Declaration of Taking. For the sake
of national security, sir, your land has been condemned.
As you know, it's needed for the expansion of the
White Sands Missile Range."

Again the old man spoke, slowly and distinctly:
"This ranch is not for sale. The Box V is not for sale."

Grandfather's temper was slowly rising but no one
would have noticed it but me. Familiar with the modes
and degrees of his wrath, I recognized the anger in his
somber face as he stared at the piece of paper in his
hand.

DeSalius seemed unconscious of the lion at his side.
"Legally speaking, Mr. Vogelin, your property has already been sold. Along with the Declaration of Taking
we have deposited, with the clerk of the District Court,
a check payable to you in the amount of sixty-five thousand dollars, the estimated monetary value of your land
and improvements."

"My ranch is not for sale."

"Yes. Yes sir." The colonel smiled at me, since the
old man appeared to be resistant to the smiles. "You
may contest the amount of compensation, Mr. Vogelin.
That is your privilege. And you may take the check
without prejudice."

"Sixty-five thousand is too much," the old man said grimly. "The place ain't worth fifty thousand. And I'm not selling and I'm not moving out and I'm not starting a court fight for more money."

DeSalius smiled. If he felt any strain he wasn't showing it yet. "Mr. Vogelin, legally speaking, the act of filing a Declaration of Taking pre-empts your property at the time of filing. You and I are now enjoying our ease on United States Government property." The colonel paused to allow his statement to penetrate. He went on: "Now as I said, we've got a court order allowing the Air Force immediate possession and entry. However, the Court will allow you a reasonable length of time in which to move your movable property and resettle your livestock. Perhaps a month or so—not more—since they tell me the calving season is over."

"I'm not moving outa here till I'm dead. Maybe not then either." As he spoke Grandfather stared hard at DeSalius and the look on his face would have made a wild bronc pause.

DeSalius smiled pleasantly. "I know how you feel, sir. I understand your feelings perfectly. It's always quite a shock to have your property pre-empted in this—"

"This is not property," the old man said. "This is my home. This ranch is my home and my life. Try to see if you can understand that, Colonel De—DeSalius."

"Why, yes sir, I think I understand. I mean, of course I understand." For the first time DeSalius revealed a trace of uncertainty. "Yes, it must be—it is quite a, quite a shock to have your property—your home taken away from you. Although you've had plenty of time, over a year, to prepare yourself for this . . . eventuality. And you are being generously compensated, you've admitted that yourself. Incidentally, the Government will pay all the costs of transporting your livestock and other belongings."

The old man growled and crumpled the official document in his hand; he tossed the wad on the colonel's lap. "You take that piece of paper, Colonel, and go away. I'm not going to co-operate."

DeSalius paused, drawing thoughtfully on his cigar. He drank some ice water. "Drink your ice water, Mr. Vogelin, it tastes pretty good. Good water you have here. Well water, I suppose." Grandfather made no reply. "I'd heard you were a difficult customer, Mr. Vogelin, but I thought you would at least be willing to listen to reason."

"I ain't heard any reasons yet."

"According to the report of our Inspection and Possession Committee, the entire missile range project may suffer a serious delay if we're held up much longer by these real estate problems. We've been trying to negotiate with you, sir, for over a year. All but you have come to terms. Your neighbors Haggard and Reese agreed to a settlement last night, did you know that?"

Grandfather scowled in disgust and looked out over the desert.

"Mr. Vogelin," DeSalius continued, "you alone and you only are holding up this project. And this project is an essential component of our national defense program. Now I understand how your emotions are involved in this place but you must understand that national security takes precedence over all other considerations. Every citizen owes his first allegiance to the nation, and all property rights"—the colonel smacked his lips with pleasure as he rolled out the rhetorical artillery—"all property rights are derived from and depend upon the sovereignty of the State. I refer you to the law of nations, to Grotius, Blackstone, Marshall. . . ."

"I've heard all that before. I have a friend who's in real estate and politics too. Like you. He's explained all this to me before." Grandfather removed his glasses, began polishing the lenses with a faded bandana. As he worked on the glasses he squinted at the colonel with his fierce eyes. "Colonel, my mind is made up. It won't do you any good to talk. This is my home. I'm not leaving. I'm never leaving. I was born here, I'm going to die here. I don't care how much money you offer me, I don't care how many court orders you throw at me, I am not leaving. And if you try to push me out—I'll resist. I'll fight."

The colonel sighed, flicked the ash off his cigar, and sighed again. Heavy sighs for a smiling man. At last, with a somewhat fainter smile, he said, "You should take your fight to the courts, Mr. Vogelin. If you want to fight go to court. This is a civilized country, not a jungle—try to have the condemnation act dismissed. You won't get anywhere but you can always try it, it might relieve your emotions. And you can sue for higher compensation—as of now the Court might still have sympathy for your case. Certainly any grand jury will be ready to listen to you. But if you resist, as you say, threaten violence or anything like that, why—why you'll get yourself into all sorts of extra difficulties, perhaps lose some of the compensation already awarded you, maybe worse. Think it over carefully, Mr. Vogelin. I must urge you to think it over carefully."

The old man said nothing. He put his glasses on and poured himself some more ice water, his hands tense but steady as rock.

I filled my glass again. It was hot and dry and very difficult there, in the 100-degree shade of the ranch-house verandah.

DeSalius did the same.

We were all thirsty, and the insane shrilling of the locusts in the brush out under the intolerable sun made us even thirstier. We drank ice water and listened to the locusts, listened to Cruzita singing quietly in the kitchen, preparing supper: beans, of course, with red chili sauce, and eggs—*huevos rancheros*—and the inevitable slabs of beef.

A calf bawled off to the west, across the sandy bed of the Salado. I looked out that way but could see no cattle. They were all shaded up under the cottonwoods and in the tamarisk. The delicate leaves of the cottonwood trees glimmered in the sunlight, trembling under the touch of the invisible, inaudible breeze. Clanking painfully, the old windmill near the house rotated on its bearings to face and catch the slight wind: the vanes creaked as they turned. Tonight the frogs would be bellowing, mad with moonlight and summertime.

DeSalius uncrossed his legs, shifting the chair. "Really no need for me to trouble you any longer, Mr. Vogelin. I've brought you what I wanted to bring you and told you what I had to tell you. But you must understand that in a case like this, involving what the Defense Department considers a military emergency, you have no chance to retain possession of your land. No chance, no chance whatsoever. The only issue yet to be decided is the exact amount of monetary compensation—if you want to make an issue of it."

He finished his glass of ice water and stood up. "I hope the whole procedure is clear to you and that you understand both the necessity and the justice of this action. If you have any questions I'd be glad to answer them, of course." Standing, he looked down at Grandfather. "Any questions?"

The old man, still sitting, looked up at him. "Yes, I have a question. Just one question. How do you think you can throw me outa here if I don't want to go?"

DeSalius laughed pleasantly. "Now, Mr. Vogelin, I'm sure it won't come to anything like that. You're too intelligent a man to make a fool of yourself. But if there is any difficulty the U.S. Marshal will attend to the details. That's his line of work. But I'm sure his services won't be necessary. After all, you're a citizen like the rest of us, you're capable of recognizing your obligations as well as your rights—in regard to the law of the land. I'll go now. It's been very nice talking to you. Thank you very much for this excellent cigar."

Getting no answer from Grandfather, the colonel looked at me. "And nice meeting you too, young man. By the way: what is your name? I don't think we've been introduced."

"Billy Vogelin Starr, sir." I tried to be polite.

"Well spoken. I like the way you speak out, young man—loud and clear. You're proud of your name, aren't you?"

"Yes I am."

"Well that's good, that's the way it should be. Goodbye, Billy." He turned back to the old man. "Goodbye to you, sir, it's been a pleasure to meet you and I've enjoyed our conversation." He nodded to each of us, turned smartly around and marched off the verandah through the dazzle of sunlight and under the spangled shade of the trees.

We watched him go, staring at his broad back, watched him climb in his gray government sedan and drive off. Shambles of dust obscured his exit: the car rumbled up the rocky road past sheds and corral, up the slope and out of sight.

Silence. I poured some more ice water. Wiped the sweat off my upper lip.

The old man gazed at the lingering dust. "What'd you think of that fella, Billy?"

"Sir?"

"What'd you think of that fella?"

"Seems like a nice guy," I said. "I wouldn't trust him as far as I could throw a horse."

Grandfather smiled. "We think the same, Billy. We think the same."

4

Well—the summer rolled on, hot and dry and beautiful, so beautiful it broke your heart to see it knowing you couldn't see it forever: that brilliant light vibrating over the desert, the purple mountains drifting on the horizon, the pink tassels of the tamarisk, the wild lonely sky, the black buzzards soaring above the whirlwinds, the thunderheads that piled up almost every afternoon trailing a curtain of rain that seldom reached the earth, the stillness of noonday, the sight of the horses rolling in the dust to wash off the sweat and flies, the glamorous sunrises that flooded plain and range with a fantastic, incredible, holy light, the cereus cactus that bloomed and closed on one night only, the moonlight slanting through the open door of my bunkhouse room, the sight and sound of cool water trickling from a spring after a long day in the heat—I could list a thousand things I saw that I'll never forget, a thousand marvels and miracles that pulled at something in my heart which I could not understand.

We got through June all right and most of July without too much trouble from the weather or DeSalius or the United States Government. Some of the cows got sick from eating larkspur up in the hills and five of them bloated up and died. That's natural. The rest pulled through and although you could hardly say they fattened at least they didn't lose weight: they grew tough and rangy and vicious. In the fall we would ship them to the Midwest for a quick feeding on corn and real grass before slaughter. That's life—for a beef cow.

Lee Mackie came out to see us every week and he and I went for long rides together in the hills. He told me stories of the old days when he was a boy and how he'd taken part in the defense of the ranch against the last raids of the Mescalero Apaches. All lies, of course, but good healthy lies, full of vigor and romance and grandeur.

Lee was at the ranch the day the United States Marshal made his entrance. The marshal came alone, dressed in a suit like an FBI agent, but bearing no arms or animosity. That was on the twentieth of July, the deadline specified in Judge Fagergren's final removal order.

The marshal got out of his car and looked over the scene, apparently not disturbed by what he saw: chickens strolling in the yard, dogs barking at his flanks, Peralta kids playing under the trees, laundry hanging on the line, Eloy Peralta patching the roof of the hayshed, Lee Mackie and I shoeing old Skilletfoot, Grandfather repairing the stirrup leathers of his saddle.

Lee and I were planning an overnight ride, to start that afternoon. The old man, of course, would no longer leave the ranch except for quick trips to town. He was afraid that the armed forces of the United States might confiscate his home the minute he turned his back.

"Well sir," the marshal said. That was all he said, for the moment. Looking around with an expression of perfectly neutral nonchalance, he took off his hat, swabbed his perspiring brow with a handkerchief, and put the hat back on. The marshal did not look much like a police officer: he was short and plump and middle-aged and sort of bow-legged; his face was bland and innocent as a pie. But no doubt he carried a chopped-off .38 under the shoulder of his baggy summer suit, and a submachine gun in the car.

"Well sir," he said again, revealing a Texas accent, "how are things going, Mr. Vogelin?" He was speaking to Lee.

Lee gave the man a hard appraisal before replying. "That's Mr. Vogelin over there." He pointed a thumb at Grandfather.

The marshal turned to the old man, unmoved by Lee's scrutiny. "Good evening, Mr. Vogelin." He said "evening." It was about four in the afternoon. "My name's Burr. The Judge sent me out to see how you were getting along."

When we heard the word "judge" we all stopped working and stared at the visitor.

"Are you the marshal?" Grandfather asked, putting down his iron needle and facing the man with a kind of weary resolution. Despite all the evidence offered by reason, the old man must have been hoping, somehow, that this meeting would never take place.

The marshal nodded. He was the marshal. "Yes sir, I'm the marshal." He reached inside his jacket and fumbled for something. I felt Lee's hand tighten on my shoulder as the same ridiculous thought struck us simultaneously: he's reaching for the handcuffs.

But no, like most visitors to the ranch in those days, the marshal pulled out a document.

"Well, Mr. Vogelin, I got this here piece of paper I'm supposed to give you." He held it out to Grandfather. Grandfather made no move to take it. The marshal pushed it closer to the old man. The old man would not lift a hand to accept it. After an embarrassing pause, the marshal drew the paper back and opened it and studied it. He studied it for a long time, apparently finding it hard to understand.

"Well, Mr. Vogelin, what this here paper is, this paper is an extension of the Order to Vacate." He raised his eyes to look at Grandfather. "I guess you knowed you was supposed to be off these premises, you and all your movable property, by today." He stopped and waited for an answer.

"I'm still here," the old man replied. "I'm not leaving. We're not leaving."

"Yeah? Well—" The marshal shrugged. "I guess the

Judge figured you'd still be around. This paper means you got two more weeks in which to vacate these premises. The Court gives you an extension even though you didn't request an extension. Two more weeks," the marshal mumbled. He seemed sleepy and bored. It was a hot afternoon. Around 102 degrees in the shade.

Grandfather said nothing. The marshal waited, saying nothing. In the silence we could all hear the maniacal singing of the locusts.

"I'm supposed to give you this paper, Mr. Vogelin." Again the man offered his authentic-looking document to John Vogelin and again the old man did not bother to accept it. The paper hung in the air between them, suspended from the fat fingers of a United States Marshal.

"You don't want it," the marshal stated.

Grandfather made no answer. We all stared at the marshal. Apathy seemed to cover him like the shade of the trees. His eyes were half closed. It seemed to me then that we were dealing with some type of idiot.

"Well, if you don't want it I'll leave it here." The marshal looked around for a place to put the piece of paper. The handiest level surface was the top of one of the corral fence posts. He set the paper there and within a few seconds the invisible breeze carried it off the post and into the corral, where it landed in the mud and dung by the water trough, disturbing two yellow butterflies.

The marshal put his hands in his pockets, shuffled his feet, and stared at the ground. "Something else I was supposed to tell you, Mr. Vogelin." He blinked his eyes and sniffed. Perhaps he had a case of hay fever. "Yes. About your livestock, Mr. Vogelin." The marshal stared at the ground, blinking. "If you don't remove them . . . we'll remove them for you. At your expense. That's what I was supposed to tell you."

"Thanks," the old man said.

"What we'll have to do, we'll have to take them to El Paso, auction them off. Whatever they bring you'll

. . . you'll get, minus the expenses." The marshal started to yawn. "You have any questions before I go, Mr. Vogelin?"

"How many men are you gonna bring with you next time?" Grandfather asked.

The marshal scratched his neck and shuffled his feet, thinking the matter over. "Gosh, I don't know, Mr. Vogelin. How many do you think I'll need?" He glanced sideways at me and Lee for a moment, and winked. We were not amused. He stared at the ground. "I guess I'll bring as many as I can round up," he said.

"You'll need more," Grandfather said.

The marshal stopped another yawn. "Well, you might be right, Mr. Vogelin. Yes sir, you might be right. We'll see. Anyway, I hope you won't be here . . . two weeks from now."

"I'll be here. Waiting for you." Grandfather's voice did not raise but filled with dark intensity. "And here's something you better understand; I'm going to shoot the first man who lays a hand on my house. Remember that. Tell it to the reporters if you want to. I'm going to kill the first man who touches my house."

The marshal shook his head sadly. "Now, Mr. Vogelin, please don't talk that way." He talked to the ground, not looking at the old man. "Mr. Vogelin, that's a serious offense, threatening an officer of the law. Please don't talk that way."

Suddenly the old man lost his temper. "Get out of here! Get off my property! You're trespassing on private property! Get out!"

Lee's fingers clutched hard at my shoulder. "John," he said softly. "Easy now. . . ."

"This is Government property now, Mr. Vogelin," the marshal said. He paused, then completed his thought. "You are the one that's trespassing, Mr. Vogelin."

"What's that?" Grandfather roared. "What did you say?"

Lee let go of my shoulder and stepped toward the

marshal. "You'd better leave, Marshal. You better leave right away." He stared at the man until the other lowered his head and looked at the ground.

"I'm leaving," the marshal said. He backed off a few steps and lifted one languid hand and made a vague motion in the air, a farewell salute. "See you fellas later, I suppose. I hope not, though. I mean, not here. Hope I see you somewhere else." He turned his back to us and shambled toward his car, a short fat asymmetrical man with flies following the seat of his pants.

We watched him get in the machine and drive away.

"A clown," Lee muttered.

"I'll kill that man if he comes bumbling and mumbling around here again," Grandfather said.

"That's what I call insolence," Lee said. "The way he acted. Clowning around with serious business. Bad manners and insolence, the worst kind of insolence."

Old Skilletfoot began to stamp and snort, still waiting for us to finish shoeing his hind feet. Lee turned his wrath upon the horse:

"Stand still there, whoa! Whoa! you miserable, rump-sprung, Roman-nosed, dude-spoiled, broom-tailed, ewe-necked—! Whoa, I say!"

And Skilletfoot obeyed.

After supper, after Cruzita had washed the dishes and gone home to her primary family, Lee and I started playing chess with my portable chess set. He didn't keep his mind on the game. Instead he argued with Grandfather on the same tedious and endless subject and I beat him easily in fourteen moves, after chopping him down to king, bishop, both knights, and a few scattered pawns.

We played another game. I beat him again. And not only was he losing the game, he was losing the argument with the old man. At least he wasn't winning the argument. We started the third game.

"No!" Grandfather thundered, cigar in hand. "No!" he roared, as he did a thousand times that summer, "this here *rancho* is not for sale. Not for sale, by Jesus!

I'm too old to move. They'll have to carry me outa here in a box, by God! And say, you think maybe I won't take a few of them Government men with me too." This being a statement and not a question.

"They're only trying to do their duty, John."

"Me too. My duty."

"There's a word for people like you," Lee said, giving me a sly grin.

"Words."

"The word is . . . anachronism."

"Anarchism?"

"About the same."

"Check," I said distinctly.

"I'm not afraid of words," the old man said. "You can call me anything you want to. So long as it's polite."

"Well hell, John, you can count on that."

"Check," I said again. "It's your move, Lee."

"I'm counting on you all the way, Lee."

"What'd you say, Billy?"

"Your king—is now—in check."

"Oh—yeah. So he is. What'll I do with him now?" Patiently I pointed to his queen. "She can save you, Lee."

"Yeah," he said, "the queen." And he looked at his wristwatch. "Getting kind of late."

Yes, it is," Grandfather said.

"Your move, Lee."

5

I believe it was about two weeks later that the Government drove off our stock.

We were returning to the ranch near sundown, the light blinding our eyes as the sun glared straight through the windshield. In the back of the pickup we carried almost fifty dollars worth of edibles—nearly all of it canned goods and dried beans. The old man was preparing for a long seige.

We also had mail:

For me, a letter from my mother. For Grandfather, a number of letters from the United States Government.

The old man was a little drunk but steering a fairly true course as we bounced along at forty miles an hour toward the entrance gate.

Grandfather pumped the brake pedal and the truck skidded over the rocks and humped to a stop. But before I got out to open the gate we realized that something was wrong—the gate was already wide open.

"What are they up to now?" the old man muttered. He drove the truck through the gateway and stopped. I climbed out to close the gate. I saw new placards made of steel shining at me from the gateposts:

PROPERTY OF U.S. GOVERNMENT
KEEP OUT

They were talking about our ranch. I tried to tear the things off with my bare hands and only broke a fingernail. The old man saw what I was doing and came out of the truck with a claw hammer in his grip. He ripped the signs off the posts and hurled them far out into the brush.

We turned back to the truck. And stopped.

A huge cloud of dust was rising above the salt flats where our main loading pens were. At the base of the dust cloud we could see the dim small figures of cattle, horses, men and machines. Through the quiet evening air came the low murmur, muted by the great distance, of animal activity.

A jeep was coming up the road from the flats, a blue Air Force jeep gleaming with the white helmets of the Air Police.

Out of habit Grandfather reached for the revolver in the dashboard compartment. Then he remembered me and lowered his hand. "We'll not do battle yet," he said, squinting into the sunlight and puffing on his cigar. "Not just yet." He put his hands on his hips and waited.

The jeep came closer, the engine whining with effort, the wheels gushing thick funnels of yellow dust, and stopped beside our truck. The driver remained at the wheel, but the captain sitting beside him got out and came toward us.

"Mr. Vogelin?" he asked, offering his right hand to my grandfather.

The old man refused the handshake. He was getting a little tired of shaking the hands of enemies. "I'm Vogelin," he said. "Get off my property."

The captain, a handsome young man, paled a bit but did not lose his poise. "I'm very sorry, sir. This is Government property."

"The hell it is," Grandfather said. "This is my home. What are you doing out there?" He pointed to the dust billowing above the flats.

"We've been expecting you, Mr. Vogelin. That's why I came to meet you. I'm sorry to have to be the one to tell you, sir, that we are under orders to round up your cattle and horses and take them off the land."

Watching the old man closely, counting on him for courage and strength, I was unable to see any change in the stony expression of his face. Except, maybe, that it got stonier. Harder than stone, maybe. The old man looked as if he might turn into some kind of metal right before my eyes.

"Those cattle are not for sale," Grandfather said slowly, looking not at the captain but at the action out on the flats. "You're loading my stock," he said.

I stared as hard as I could and saw through the dust the big trucks lining the road near the central loading chute. Six, seven, eight trucks—I couldn't tell for sure.

"Yes sir," the captain said. "All the trucks are loaded now but one."

"You knew I was gone."

"Yes sir. We were under orders to do it this way."

Still not looking at the captain, Grandfather said: "Sort of a cowardly way to do it, wouldn't you say?"

This time the captain did not flinch. "Yes sir," he said, "I agree with you. But—" He stopped, hesitated.

"There seems to be so damned *many* of you people," the old man said. "Every other day a new—face." Abruptly he diverted the course of thought. "What happened to Eloy? You'd have to kill him to get away with this."

"Eloy?" the captain said. "Eloy . . . ? You mean Eloy Peralta?"

"Eloy Peralta," Grandfather said. He stared at the loading operations through the dust and cruel glare of the sun.

"If you mean your hired hand, Peralta—" The captain paused to lick the sweat from his upper lip. "—If you mean Peralta, I'm afraid I have to tell you that he's under arrest. In fact he's already in jail. He gave us a little trouble this morning. . . ."

"I should've stayed home," Grandfather said. "I should've let Lee bring the. . . ." Louder, he said, "Is he all right?"

"Is who all right, sir?"

"Is Eloy all right?"

"Yes, Mr. Vogelin, he didn't get hurt. Nobody got hurt, actually. We're trying to keep this a clean, decent courteous operation."

The captain's irony was wasted on my grandfather. The old man would not smile, would not even look at the man. Grandfather kept his eyes averted, as though something unclean stood before him. After a considerable and significant silence he turned to me. "Let's go, Billy."

The officer shifted nervously. "You're not going to attempt to interfere, are you, Mr. Vogelin?"

The armed man at the wheel of the jeep kept his small pink eyes focused on us, a twitchy irritable grin on his mouth. A second Air Policeman sat in the back seat. He too watched us with shiny eyes and a face shiny with sweat.

The pair of them sitting there in the jeep, sweating, silent, motionless, holstered automatics on their wide hips, gave me a sensation of nausea.

"No," Grandfather said. He climbed into the pickup truck and I got in beside him.

"I must request that you do not interfere," the captain said quite seriously, stepping close to the truck and placing one restraining hand on the windowless window frame. "You understand, Mr. Vogelin, I am under orders to prevent any kind of interference with the property in this, ah, this transaction. The procedure is entirely legal."

"Legal thievery," the old man said. He started the engine. "Legal thievery. No," he added, shifting into low gear, "I won't interfere. Take the poor beasts. Take them all, they're starving anyway. But don't try to send me any money. I don't take money from thieves." He engaged the clutch and we moved off. Looking back through the window I saw the captain step briskly to the jeep and get into it. They were going to follow us.

The sun went down, suddenly, as we approached the flat. The first of the big cattle trucks came toward us, headlights burning through the dust and twilight. Behind the first came others—one, two, three, four, five, siv. Grandfather turned off the road. We halted to watch the fleet go by. Each truck carried about twenty-five head of cattle, the last of the Box V herd.

One of the truckdrivers waved at us as he went by. "Hi, John," he shouted.

Grandfather was looking elsewhere.

The trucks rumbled by, each loaded with living flesh —I had glimpses of the brown flanks and the rolling eyeballs through the grating of the vans, and heard the bawling of the calves.

After the trucks came a half-ton pickup with a pair of saddle horses—not ours—in the racked bed and two strange cowhands sitting up front. They gave us a sullen greeting; we ignored them. After that another Air Force jeep appeared, layered with dust, loaded with dusty airmen. They stared at us as we stared at them.

We were ready to go on home when the first jeep came alongside and the captain got out and came to see us again, though nobody was looking for him. His clean-cut well-intentioned face confronted us through the open window at Grandfather's side.

We ignored him for a while.

He said, "Mr. Vogelin?"

Grandfather did not reply.

"Mr. Vogelin," the captain said. "I'd like to apologize for my part in this sorry business. I'm really ashamed of the whole thing and didn't want any part of it, but—but I couldn't get out of it." The captain smiled, a wistful smile. "I work for the Government. I have to do what I'm told."

"No, you don't," Grandfather said.

"Will you accept my apology, sir?"

For the first time Grandfather looked at the man. "Don't worry about it, son. But please get off my ranch and don't ever come back."

The captain's face vanished as Grandfather stepped on the gas pedal and the truck leaped ahead. The old man didn't look back once, but I did. I looked back and watched the caravan of trucks and jeeps winding toward the east under planes of golden dust, taking away the heart of my grandfather's life.

"Hope they remember to close the gate," the old man said softly.

Why? I thought. We don't need gates now. We don't need fences. I wanted to cry. I found it difficult not to cry, but resolved to wait until I was alone. If Grandfather would not weep, neither would I.

There was a spectacular sunset over the mountains that evening—a bright, gay circus of scarlet clouds and radiant sky. The spectacle filled me with disgust.

We reached the ranch-house and parked close to the front door to unload our war supplies. Cruzita sat on the verandah with her five children, waiting for us. She began to sob as we walked heavily toward her.

"Meestair Vogelin!" she cried. "Meestair Vogelin!" and she staggered toward the old man, wiping her lovely face on her apron.

Grandfather stroked her shoulders. "Don't cry, Cruzita, it's all right. We ain't whipped yet." She continued to bawl, leaning against him. "Please don't cry," he said gently. "Fix us something to eat. We're hungry. The boy's hungry."

The liar. I had no appetite either. No appetite for anything but war and revenge.

The children, brown and dirty, solemn as a row of owls, sat quietly and watched us.

"It's all ready," Cruzita said. "I warm it up a little now." She turned and led the way into the house and into the kitchen, the old man and I following with our boxes of battle rations. The house was dark and cool, full of somber shadows, filled with an air of regret, of disaster.

Grandfather lit a pair of kerosene lamps as Cruzita stirred up beans, potatoes, meat, tacos, enchiladas and coffee over the blue flames of the gas burner. "You sit down," she said. "I feed you."

We washed some of the dust off our hands and faces under the tap. The water felt lukewarm from being all day in the tank. We sat down at the table as Cruzita piled food on our plates.

"My Eloy," she blubbered, standing over us with the pot, "he try to stop them, Meestair Vogelin. But they was so many. He could do nothing. They arrest him, take him to town, put him in the jail, I think."

"I know, Cruzita," Grandfather said. "We'll go back to town tonight and bail him out." He fiddled with his supper. "But you and Eloy can't stay here any more. You'll have to leave until this business is settled."

I didn't care for the sound of that remark. And I could guess easily enough what was in my mother's letter: *School begins in three weeks. Come home at once.*

Cruzita objected, of course, to Grandfather's command, and swore that she and Eloy would not leave him, would fight to the end. So Grandfather said he'd let Eloy rot in the county jail instead, if that's the way she wanted it. And he ordered her to pack her things and be ready to go in an hour. Cruzita refused. The old man bellowed at her. Finally she backed down and left the kitchen, sobbing and protesting, and went off to her own house with the children trotting beside her.

"Where is Lee?" Grandfather said quietly to me.

I was wondering the same thing. We forced some grub down our reluctant gullets, got up, piled the dishes in the sink (but not for Cruzita this time) and brought in the remainder of our supplies from the truck.

The old man set about fortifying the house. We closed all the heavy wooden shutters and hooked them on the inside. We bolted and barred the kitchen door and the back door and stacked mattresses against both, supporting the mattresses in place with tables, chairs and bedsteads. We filled the washtub and all of our buckets, mason jars, and rum jugs with water, in case the enemy should try to cut the waterline from the tank outside. We left the main entrance open, for the time

being, since we still expected a few hours or even days
to pass before the seige began.

There was not much more we could do for the present. The old man sent me off to Peralta's house to see
if Cruzita was ready.

I'd enjoyed the military preparations—they seemed
so practical—but this child's errand annoyed me. As I
stumbled through the August gloom under the whispering cottonwood trees, remotely aware of the night-
hawk's booming over the wash, I resolved to do something dramatic and significant. I wasn't sure what. First
of all I'd steal that revolver out of the truck again and
make sure it remained in my possession. That would be
a beginning.

I passed the corral. Three horses waited there, hoping for grain. There was Blue and Skilletfoot and
Grandfather's stallion, Rocky. The others were gone.

I entered Peralta's house through the open front
door, into a hot, crowded lamplit room where Cruzita
sat among a litter of cardboard boxes and ancient suit-
cases. She was packing a trunk with clothes and household utensils. The holy pictures still hung on the walls:
Jesus with his bleeding heart; the Madonna and child,
obvious gringo types; and a tinted photograph of the
Pope with miter and crozier.

Cruzita still wept a little as she worked, but I noticed
that she'd washed her face and brushed her hair, and
that the children, running around through the trans-
formed house, looked clean and neat. She could accept
the inevitable: Grandfather and I could not.

I wondered where she would go. As I helped her
finish stuffing the trunk she volunteered the information: she and the children would stay with relatives in
El Paso until Mr. Vogelin sent for them; Eloy would
work for his brother, who owned a small bar and pack-
age store in Las Cruces, only twenty miles from El
Paso. They'd manage.

I heard a car coming down over the *barrancas*. I left
Cruzita, ran outside and watched the car come near. It

was Lee in his big automobile. The lights washed over
the yard, swung past the corral and the shining eyes of
the horses and came to a bead on Grandfather's pickup
as the car stopped. The lights went out. I ran to greet
him.

He looked pretty serious but gave me a smile as I
grabbed his arm. "Hi, Billy, what're you all excited
about? Where's the old man?"

"In the house. Gosh, Lee, I'm glad you came."

He put his arm around my shoulders. "I hope I'm
not too late, Billy."

We went in the house and found Grandfather by the
fireplace in the parlor, cleaning his shotgun and carbine
by the light of the kerosene lamps.

"This looks like war," Lee said, with a tired smile.

Grandfather grunted some kind of answer as he drew
a clean white patch from the bore of the carbine. With
the action open he held the gun up to the light and
peered through the barrel. "Where you been?" he said.

"What? I just heard about it," Lee said. "Those dirty
rotten. . . . John, I want to tell you, I want to tell you
that's the lousiest dirtiest trick I ever heard of. Cowardly and sneaky. Something like this ought to be written up in every paper in the country. Maybe it will be.
Maybe if we get enough publicity we'll scare off the Air
Force yet. Stranger things have happened."

Grandfather said nothing—just broke open the
double-barreled shotgun.

"We don't need publicity," I said, horning in where
I knew I wasn't needed. "We need ammunition." I remembered the revolver in the truck. I started toward
the door.

"Stay here, Billy," the old man said. "Keep your
little paws off that revolver."

Lee came nearby and patted my shoulder. "He's a
good boy, John. You ought to be mighty grateful to
have a boy like this around."

The old man squinted through the shotgun barrels
at the lamplight. "Look pretty good," he muttered. But

he threaded a new patch through the eye of the cleaning rod.

A short silence as we watched him at work: Lee said, "I suppose you're sure this is what you want to do. Fight them off with guns, I mean."

"Well . . ." Grandfather grinned slyly at Lee. "It's traditional."

Lee paused again before speaking. "Are you really planning to—you really expect an attack?" He looked at the barricaded windows.

"They drove nearly all my stock off today," the old man said. "I expect I'm next." He looked around for me. "Cruzita ready?"

"Yes sir. Just about."

Grandfather turned his face to Lee. "You want to help me some tonight?"

Lee lifted his hands in a gesture of surprise. "Why do you think I'm here?"

"Just asking. Well, if you want to help me, how about taking Cruzita and her kids to town and bailing out Eloy and putting them all on the El Paso bus. No, I have a better idea. Take them all direct to El Paso. Them—and something else."

I stood up.

"Sit down, Billy," Grandfather said.

I sat down. The front door stood open; moths and millers swarmed against the screen.

"Okay," Lee said. "You mean tonight?"

"Right away. Right now."

"You staying here?"

"That's right. I left this ranch for the last time today. I learned my lesson. Next time I leave it'll be in a box, feet first, unless the Government gets off my back."

"They won't." Lee glanced uneasily at me. "Billy . . ."

"Take him," the old man said. "Pack him on the train. And make sure—"

"Wait a minute," I howled, rising again.

"Make sure he's still on that train when it leaves."

"No," I cried. "No. I won't go. I want to stay. Please, Grandfather."

"His suitcase is in the hallway," Grandfather said. "All packed. Take him out of here, Lee."

"Sure." Lee looked at me again, smiling but obviously embarrassed. "Guess you're going home, Billy."

"Please," I shouted, "please, Grandfather, don't make me go. Not now. You need me. I want to help. Please."

"Get your suitcase, Billy," he said.

"I'll get it." Lee strode out of the room, returning in aa moment with my bag in his hand. "Is everything in here?" he asked both of us.

"I didn't pack it," I said bitterly.

"It's all in there," the old man said. "All his gear. Take him, Lee. If you need a rope there's a rope in the pickup."

"My hat," I said weakly. I took my rotten and crumpled straw hat off the deer horns by the fireplace. And reconsidered. "I'm not going," I said. "Sir, I'm not going. You can't make me go, Grandfather."

The old man laid the shotgun on the table. Leaning on his hands, he looked me over carefully. The cigar stub was still in his mouth. "What did you say, Billy? Maybe I ain't hearing so good tonight."

"Come on, Billy," Lee said, while I gaped at Grandfather, framing a plea in my mind. Good God, what could I say? I was numb with shock and disappointment and the feeling of helplessness.

Lee wrapped his big fingers gently around my upper arm. "You're under arrest, Billy. Let's go."

"Sorry I can't offer you a drink tonight, Lee," Grandfather said. "I could but I think we ought to get these women and children off the place and get Eloy out of jail as soon as possible."

"He's been there plenty of times before," Lee said. "I know."

"What do you mean," I burst out, "Women and children? I'm no child. Don't call me a child, sir."

"He didn't mean you, Billy."

"I meant the woman and children and Billy Vogelin Starr," Grandfather said. "Excuse me."

Lee increased his pressure on my arm and nudged me toward the door. I leaned forward. My legs seemed to be paralyzed. "You want me to carry you?" Lee asked.

My legs came slowly alive. "I'll walk. Gimme that suitcase." I took the heavy bag from Lee's hand, crammed the hat on my head and started forward, lugging the weight. Before pushing open the screen door I stopped for a final appeal to the old man. His back was turned to me and he looked bulky as a bear. "Grandfather . . ." I began.

"Goodbye, Billy." He wouldn't look at me.

Suddenly I dropped the suitcase, ran to him, hugged him around the waist and began to blubber. The old man squeezed my shoulder, kissed me on the forehead and shoved me roughly toward Lee.

"Send him home, Lee. Please get him out of here."

Lee grabbed me and grabbed my suitcase and together we stumbled out of the house and into the night. We felt our way to the big car under the trees. Beyond the leaves hung a sea of shimmering stars. Lee pushed me into the car and slammed the door. We drove to Cruzita's house.

6

By the time we got Eloy out of jail and drove the sixty miles to El Paso it was too late to catch the night train. Lee and I walked across the international bridge over the Rio Grande, inspected some of the Juarez night life, walked back into El Paso and spent the night in a hotel room. My train was due to leave at nine-twenty in the morning.

I couldn't sleep that night. Several times I got up and padded to the bathroom and padded back to my bed. Each time I noticed Lee watching me with a wary eye.

We ate a sad breakfast in the hotel coffee shop and drove down to the Southern Pacific depot to wait for the train. Lee and I seemed to have little to say to each other that morning. In silence we walked around the lobby, studying the people, the magazines on the newsstand and the train schedules above the ticket windows. I hoped that train would never arrive. I hoped it would break down in Tucson or Deming, would fall into the river at Las Cruces. But it came.

Lee led me along with the mob out to the tracks and down past the aluminum cars to the car I was to ride in. The porter in his dark-blue suit stood waiting for us at the steps to the vestibule. Lee showed him my ticket, we entered the train and I climbed up on the seat and stowed my suitcase in the baggage rack. While I was getting tentatively settled in my place I noticed Lee talking to the porter and putting money in his hand—several green bills.

Outside the conductor looked once more at his gold

Hamilton on the gold chain. "All aboooord!" he yelped.

Lee came to me. "Goodbye, Billy. Now shake hands and—see you next year."

He smiled down at me with that warm and handsome smile that always soothed my heart. We shook hands, he gave me a parting slap on the shoulder, turned and strode down the corridor out of sight.

I looked out the window as the train lurched forward. Lee was there, tall and slim in the crowd of Texans and Mexicans lining the platform. He took off his big hat and waved it at me as my car rolled past. I waved back and watched him, the people around him, and the station buildings slide away into the lost past.

Lost? Not yet. Not for me.

The conductor and porter stood in the rear of the car, talking. About me, perhaps; it seemed to me that they were each watching me with one eye. Even so I got up out of my seat and walked to the forward end of the car. I felt the eyes of the porter following me as I pushed open the door of the men's toilet.

In there, alone, I looked out through the window at the greasy slums and freight yards of El Paso gliding by. We were already rolling fast, eastward bound, and I knew I'd have to jump this train quickly if I didn't want to end up in the deserts of West Texas.

After waiting another minute or two, I stepped out of the toilet. The porter and conductor, though still facing me, were looking at a sheaf of papers in the conductor's hand. I pushed through the door to the vestibule, into the roaring tent between cars, and looked about for the red-handled lever.

EMERGENCY STOP

I found it at once, above the brakeman's wheel. I wrapped my first around the handle and pulled it all the way down.

Nothing happened. For a moment. And then the air brakes hit and the great wheels locked and screeched like banshees as the train slid forward over dry hot steel. I felt the coupling buckle beneath the deck I stood on, felt the whole train shuddering and twisting under the violence of the collision between velocity and mass. Through the glass of the vestibule door I saw the conductor lumbering toward me, his face red as a tomato. I opened the outer door, saw the cinders and tie ends moving past below, but not too fast.

I closed my eyes and leaped. I hit the ground with a numbing shock, and rolled ahead several times with the momentum of the train. When I stopped rolling I opened my eyes, found I was still alive, got up and began running. A clamor of shouts burst out behind me. I ran across the gleaming tracks in front of the advance of a whistling switch engine, stumbled and fell, got up again and kept on running, headed for the cyclone fence at the edge of the yards.

I reached the fence and climbed it with my fingers and the pointed toes of my cowboy boots, rolled over three strands of barbed wire at the top and dropped to the ground, leaving shreds of my coat and pants behind. I heard the whistles of the railroad bulls but nothing like that could stop me. Still running, I dashed across the street between fast-moving trucks and up a narrow alley.

My wind was coming hard now, my ribs ached with the sharp pain of my effort, but I would not stop. Past the garbage cans, over a sleeping wino, I kept going until I reached the next street, turned the corner and slowed to a walk, panting like a dog.

I saw a bus veer off to stop a block ahead. I tried to run again but could not and the bus pulled away before I reached the stop. There were a few people on the sidewalks — Negroes, Mexicans, hungover cowboys. None of them paid me any attention. I glanced back, saw no sign of pursuit. At the next corner I turned again, walking as fast as I could away from the railroad, and looked for a place to hide and rest.

Another alleyway. I stepped into it, comforted by

the close walls, the backsides of flophouses, cafés, beer joints and small shops. A stairway led down to a cellar door. I stumbled down the steps and collapsed in a heap against the steel door, closing my eyes and pretending I was invisible.

Several minutes passed and I began to breathe normally again. I opened my eyes. A man in blue overalls walked by above, saw me, gave me a hesitant glance, passed on his way. I stayed where I was, till the door at my back was opened abruptly from within and I fell down on my side.

A Negro in jeans and coffee-colored T-shirt, a huge carton on his shoulder, stared down at me. "You're in my way, sonny."

I rolled aside and he stepped over my legs, climbed the steps with his burden and disappeared.

I got up, brushed myself off a little, combed my hair with my fingers, reshaped my crushed straw hat, and walked up the stairway to street level. When I reached the sidewalk I stopped, bewildered and uncertain of my direction. I felt completely disoriented. Then I realized that the morning sun, blazing hot through the city's smog and dust, was shining in my face. I turned my back to the sun and proceeded westward in a direction which paralleled the railway, now two or three blocks to the south. I had no sure idea where the bus terminal might be but guessed that it was probably in the center of the city, somewhere near the train station.

As I walked on, bruised and tired but vaguely elated, I did not forget to watch for the inevitable police patrol car. When the first one appeared, two blocks ahead, I stepped into the doorway of a bar. Three men on barstools eyed me as I came in; the bartender, a skinny young woman with her hair done up in paper curlers, frowned at me. But before she said anything the patrol car passed and I stepped outside again into the fierce heat of the forenoon. The reflection of myself in a window suggested that the straw cowboy hat might be a giveaway in the eyes of a conscientious cop. I dropped the hat in a trash can as I went on.

I was afraid to ask anyone for directions. I walked on and on, bearing westward through the depths of El Paso toward the island of skyscrapers at the center. The traffic increased, the sidewalks became crowded, and I became aware of the new aspect of the people around me—not so many cowboys and Mexicans, more ruddy-faced Texans in tropical-weave suits and throngs of bright blue-eyed blonde women wearing sheath skirts, their calves golden in nylon and their feet in spike-heeled shoes—strange, alarming creatures who seemed unable to see me as I plodded along beneath their shoulders.

A cop on foot patrol rounded the corner ahead, carrying his stick. I sidled into a women's hat shop, where slim things with elegant limbs cackled at one another like hens above the continuous murmur of the air-conditioning system. A scowling and richly-painted face of an indeterminate sex lowered at me as I trod on the deep carpeting. I backed to the door and slipped out behind the policeman's back.

Finally I decided I'd have to use my powers of speech if I were ever to find the bus station. Otherwise I might walk clear through the city and have to come back again. I stopped in front of an ancient little man selling papers at the curb; though he looked ninety years old he was not as tall as I. He told me where the bus station was. I followed the street pointed out by his crooked finger and sure enough, when I walked down it, there was the Greyhound in neon, the familiar smell of diesel fumes, the usual assembly of homesick draftees and sailor boys.

I counted my money, bought a one-way ticket to Baker, and decided to have some lunch. Climbing onto a stool at the counter I ordered two hamburgers with everything, a chocolate milkshake and a wedge of apple pie with ice cream. I'd missed this sort of soft sweet rotten food out at Grandfather's ranch.

As I ate my lunch I kept an eye on the mirror behind the lunch counter, watching the traffic that passed through the doorways. If any policeman appeared I was resolved to bolt for the men's room. But no one bothered me.

My bus, bound for Albuquerque by way of Baker, Alamogordo, Carrizozo and Socorro, would not leave for another two hours. When I'd finished eating I decided to hide in the john.

I sat in there for a long time, locked in a booth and reading a newspaper to pass the time. When I tired of that I recalled in detail my escape from the train and my progress through the city. I wondered if Lee could have heard about it yet and decided that that was unlikely. If he knew he'd guess immediately where I was headed for and how, and the next feet I'd see, through the opening under the toilet door, would be his in their rich brown boots, and the next voice I'd hear would be Lee Mackie's, calling out my name:

Billy! Billy Vogelin Starr!

I shook my head, woke up. A memory of a dream floated through my mind and then was lost. I heard the rumble of the loudspeaker calling off old names: Alamogordo, Carrizozo, Socorro . . .

I jumped up, suddenly alert and panicky, fumbled with the doorlatch, escaped, and walked as fast as I could, without running, out of the men's room, through the lobby and out to Gate Three, where the bus waited for me, silver door still open, the driver punching the ticket of the last passenger in the queue. I trotted up, he looked me over closely, and accepted my ticket with what seemed to me like distrust.

"Where are you going, boy?"

I swallowed once before speaking. "Baker." Couldn't he read the ticket?

"No baggage?"

"What?"

"Where's your baggage?"

"I—don't have any."

"Baker, eh?"

"Yes sir."

"You live there?"

"Yes. Yes sir."

Reluctantly he gave me back my perforated ticket. For a second we both held it, tugging gently against each other. "What're you doing in the big city all by yourself?" he asked.

"Sir?"

"I said. . . ." He stopped, sighed, shrugged his narrow shoulders. "Hop in, sonny."

I found a seat well in the rear of the bus, among the Negroes and Mexicans, behind the soldiers and sailors and Southern-type women. A short spell later we were all riding luxuriously and safely through traffic-jammed streets toward the north, toward the desert, toward freedom and war.

When the bus halted an hour later before Hayduke's combination post office, grocery store and bus stop in Baker, in the middle of the afternoon, I still had not figured out where I could hide through the remainder of the endless August day.

Two people were getting out of the bus. I followed close behind them and as they entered Hayduke's place I entered too. Fortunately for me no one was waiting on customers except old man Hayduke himself, and he was busy sorting mail behind the post-office grill.

The two strangers went up to him; I sneaked on by and into the men's room. I locked the door, climbed on the sink and looked out the small half-open window.

Nothing much to see: an open lot extending clear to a fence half a mile away, the lot traversed by a dirt road at the moment empty of traffic. I could not possibly wander out that way without being seen by somebody. And as I understood my plan, I had to get back to the ranch undetected and keep in hiding there too, until the crucial day arrived when the old man would need me.

A customer tried to open the toilet door, found it locked, swore, and went away. But he'd be back, or others would. I looked up to the ceiling and found what I had hoped for: a trap door. By standing on the water closet on top of the toilet bowl I was able to reach and open it. But before pulling myself up into the blackness of the attic I unlocked the entrance to the room, after making sure no one was waiting on the other side of the door. It seemed best.

Quickly, before anyone did come, I hoisted myself up through the ceiling and put the trap door back in place.

Black as night up in there and nothing to rest on but the ceiling joists, A rack of two-by-fours makes a poor bed. I waited for my eyes to get used to the darkness, then looked around.

A few feet away was a door in the attic partition. I went through that and found myself in Hayduke's loft, which was lit by a window overlooking the main street of Baker. This was a considerable improvement. Also the loft was floored and contained a few pieces of junk furniture. Except for the smothering heat, there was little to complain of. I sat down near the window and after watching the near-empty street for a while, fell asleep.

I woke up around sundown, craving water, my belly grumbling for food. The close air and heat made me feel nauseated as well. I listened carefully for any sound of activity in the store and post office below. There was none. Undoubtedly old Hayduke had gone home hours before. I opened another hatch, much bigger than the trap door over the men's room, and climbed down a wooden ladder nailed to the wall.

One dim electric bulb glowed in the post office behind the wall of mailboxes, barely modifying the twilight that filled the store. A man clomped past in front, boots clattering on the concrete. I crept on hands and knees to the soft-drink cooler and helped myself to a bottle of orange soda pop. That helped. I drank a second, then crawled to the bakery goods and ate six chocolate cupcakes, which aroused my thirst again.

I crept back to the cooler and drank two more bottles of orange pop.

This was thievery, of course. After a great struggle with my conscience I decided not to leave any money on Hayduke's cash register. Not because I couldn't afford it—I had nearly ten dollars left—but chiefly because it gave me such a deep authentic pleasure to steal. I ate more cupcakes, drank more pop, and waited for the night to settle in.

When it did I crawled on all fours to the rear door and slipped out into the cool blessed darkness. For the first time in five hours I was able and felt free to stand upright.

The open lot faced toward the east. I walked south behind the scattered buildings of Baker, crossed the highway half a mile south of town and headed northwest toward the dirt road that led to Vogelin's ranch.

Perhaps my direction was a little off course. Though I had the lights of the town to guide me it was an hour before I reached the road. And by that time I was hungry and thirsty again. I cursed myself for stupidly forgetting to bring any of Hayduke's food and drink with me. Too late now.

I struck out west at a steady walk, feeling light as a tumbleweed, despite my hunger and thirst, or maybe because of it. Gaily I tramped along, watching the maneuvers of the stars, and one by one sang all the new songs that Lee had taught me that summer. There'd be no moon tonight, but my night vision was good. The road stretched out ahead as clear to me as an illuminated highway.

It wasn't long though before I started to tire. I lay down in the sandy ditch and rested and slept for I don't know how long, till the cold night air chilled me through and I woke up and walked on.

A jet plane roared far overhead, the afterburner glowing like a red star. Presently I heard another noise, the sound of an automobile. I looked back and saw a pair of lights twinkling on my trail, bobbing toward me on the uneven road.

Panicked, I ran off the road and into a barbed wire fence. The flat open desert surrounded me. No place to hide. I crawled through the fence, tearing my coat again, and ran away from the road and hid behind a clump of saltbush, stretching prone on the sand. A shrill buzzing started nearby. For a moment I didn't understand it. I suppose I unconsciously assumed it was a locust, but when I saw the dark coils and the spade-shaped head rising beyond my outstretched hand I understood quickly enough, without any thinking about it, and rolled away and ran for the next saltbush, and threw myself down again.

The car swept past, taillights shining through the dust. Lee's car? I couldn't be sure; it might have been. I got up and started toward the road. It was then that the terror hit me, the full meaning of that vibrating rope of poison. I had to sit down and rest some more before my heart finally stopped thumping like an engine and my nerves had composed themselves enough to resume control of my muscles and limbs.

Tired as a branded calf, I crawled through the barbed wire and wobbled down the road, following the fading hum of the car and the tiny red lights. The lights soon disappeared and the sound of the motor petered out completely. Under the silence of the stars I plodded on, my head drooping and my arms hanging dead, my hands heavy as rocks.

Hours later—it seemed like hours later—I saw the boundary line of grandfather's ranch, the big square gateway looming black against the deep blue of the night. I was almost upon it before I saw the jeep parked near the gate, the gleam of helmets, the burning coal of a cigarette, and heard the mumble of human voices, the static of radio.

I stopped, stared, almost too dazed by hunger and thirst and fatigue to care now whether I was caught or not. At last I decided not to give up, not yet, and walked a big detour around the jeep and the gateway, climbing over a couple of fences and angling back to the road well beyond the guards.

At least I had learned where I was. Ranch head-quarters—home, food, water and sleep—were only three miles farther. That knowledge gave me the courage to continue. Shuffling through the dust, stumbling over the teeth of buried ledges of rock, I marched on, dreaming of water and meat—yes, it was meat I yearned for now—and a hidden corner in which to lie down and sleep for a few days.

Headlights emerged from the Salado wash and leveled at me, coming across the old lakebed. Once more I hurried off the road and lay down behind the brush, first making sure there was no rattlesnake waiting for me. The car approached, racing across the alkali flats and then slowing as it climbed and wound up the slope among the boulders. I watched it come, too tired to be more than mildly curious. But this time I was sure it was Lee's car and I thought I saw two men on the front seat. That meant that Grandfather had abandoned the ranch-house to join in the search for me.

It seemed to take another hour for me to comprehend what that might mean. When awareness came at last it was too late. I stood up, ran toward the road, and howled with all my strength at the receding taillights:

"Grandfather! Lee! Stop! Wait! Grandfather. . . !"

Too late: the car kept going, the lights faded in the distance. How could they have heard me? Tears streamed down my face as I stood helplessly in the middle of the road and watched the lights of the car merge with the darkness, and heard the whine of the motor grow thinner and thinner, spiraling up and out-ward into the roofless sky.

What could I do now? I didn't know. I couldn't think of a thing. I turned toward the flats, trudged on, on and on, down the slope, across the mile-wide dry lake, past the big corrals and loading pens, up the ridge beyond and then down the last winding mile of the road to the Salado and the ranch buildings.

When I finally got there I was too tired to eat. Instead of going to the house I headed straight for the corral and barn, still bound by the idea that I must hide.

I rolled through the rails of the corral, drank my fill from the trickling pipe at the head of the water trough, and staggered into the harness and saddle room.

The last thing I saw, before wrapping myself in a saddle blanket and crumbling to the straw on the floor, was the pale band of the dawn over the *barranca*. My eyelids closed, my head stopped spinning, the tears dried out on my cheeks, and the world, the whole wide world with its mountains and police and lions and horses and women and men melted away like a dream.

7

The mockingbird clattered like a crow outside the window. Sunlight streamed in massive dusty bars through the room, coming from the west. When I opened my eyes and found myself in my bed in the bunkhouse I was not at all surprised. Nothing could have seemed more natural. But when I remembered what had happened the day before and what would happen today, I rolled quickly out of bed and reached for my clothes, draped over the chair.

As I dressed I became aware of low voices on the bench outside, under the shade of the cottonwoods. I heard my grandfather; I heard Lee Mackie. I had no recollection whatsoever of being carried in here, but I did remember that I'd gone to sleep in the barn under a saddle blanket.

Stepping cautiously to the door, I opened it a crack and peeked outside. There they were, the old man smoking his cigar, Lee whittling on a stick and talking to him. The sun was close to the peak of Thieves' Mountain—I'd slept through the entire day.

My stomach rumbled like a bear. I was ferociously hungry. And frightened too. I didn't know how I could face the old man's wrath and I couldn't see how I might escape it. It didn't occur to me to try to hide again. Too late for that sort of foolishness now. After a long hesitation, and impelled more by hunger than by bravery, I opened the door and walked out.

I stood there, blinking in the evening glare.

"Hungry, Billy?" That was the first thing Grandfather said to me.

"Yes sir."

"Your supper's ready in the ranch-house. On the stove. Go wash your face, get your hair combed, eat, and come back out here. We want to talk to you."

"Yes sir." I moved dully toward the house. Lee had smiled at me but the old man looked very stern.

In the dark barricaded kitchen I cleaned myself up a little, very quickly and very little, and took the covered tin plate off the stove. Beans, meat, fried potatoes. I gobbled it all down in two minutes and helped myself to seconds out of the cast-iron pot. Drank about a quart of water and ate some more potatoes. At last I felt strong enough to go out again and face my punishment.

The two men stopped their conversation as I approached.

The sun was out of sight by now and the bats and nighthawks were at work. In the purple twilight you couldn't be too sure of anything.

"Sit down, Billy," Grandfather said.

I sat down. Lee put his big warm hand on my knee. "You sure gave us a scare, old horse," he said. "We had all the cops and sheriff's deputies of six counties looking for you yesterday. If you ever try any damn fool thing like that again why we're through, old buddy, we're not inviting you to New Mexico again."

"I'm sorry," I said. And paused. "I won't do it again." And paused again. "I just had to get back here."

"It's a good thing we spotted your tracks last night. We saw where you detoured around the guards and came meandering down the road. We might be down in El Paso right now looking for you and the Air Force would be swarming all over this place."

I was too ashamed to say anything.

"We didn't tell your mother," Lee went on. "And that's another good thing for you. If she ever hears about this she'll never let you out of her sight again and you know it."

I knew it and kept silent.

Grandfather grunted, cleared his throat, removed the cigar for a moment. "I'm gonna let you stay one more week, Billy. Just one more week. Then you're going home. Understand?"

"Yes sir."

We all fell silent. I listened to the bats clicking, the rush of the nighthawks, the nervous clucking of the chickens as they went to roost for the night in the hay-shed. I heard the hooves of our last three horses in the corral as they came in for water.

"Well, I ought to get home," Lee said. "Supper'll be cold and Annie's going to be mad at me again."

"You ought to treat her good, Lee," the old man said. "You got a good woman, treat her good."

"You can count on that." Lee sighed, stretching himself, and made an effort to stand up. "By God I'm tired. These last twenty-four hours just about got me licked."

"Might have some more excitement in the next day or two," Grandfather said.

"You can count on that too. I'll be waiting. Just give me the word when you need me. I'll be out again some-time tomorrow anyway. Why the hell don't you get a telephone, John?"

"I never learned how to talk in them things."

"You could learn."

"Sure, I could learn. But I don't want to get tangled up in telephone wire. I got enough trouble."

Lee smiled and squeezed my shoulder. "You take care of this old crank, Billy. Maybe it's a good thing you did come back."

He stood up slowly, stretching his six feet and two inches toward the limbs of the tree, while I watched in dumb admiration. His gabardine suit was dusty and rumpled, his tie was loose, his new hat was already showing sweat stains, but still he looked like a gentle-man and a Westerner. I'd have voted for Lee anytime.

"Wish I could stay," he said.

"You go home and be nice to your wife. Get some sleep."

"You're right. Absolutely right. So long, you two. See you tomorrow." He turned reluctantly away and walked, straight and tall, toward his lustrous automobile. If he was really tired he didn't show it much.

The world grew darker as we watched Lee drive away. The old man unwrapped a fresh cigar.

"Grandfather," I asked, "what're those men doing in the jeep out by the east gate?"

"They're guarding me," he said, smiling. He lit the cigar. As he puffed on it the gnats withered away in our vicinity. "They're there to keep people out, I guess. Reporters and sightseers and such. Lee says we're in the newspapers now."

"What will they do next?"

"Who?"

"The Government."

"I don't know. Maybe tomorrow we'll find out." He puffed on the powerful cigar. "You know, Billy, your aunts want me to sell out. I got letters from all of them the other day. Even your mother wants me to sell out."

"My mother!" For a moment I was too shocked to say more. "Aw no, Grandfather, not Mother. She wouldn't. Not Mother. No sir. Maybe my father . . ."

"The letter is in your mother's handwriting, Billy."

"I don't care. No sir, I don't believe it. Why, she wouldn't ever—I'll bet my father . . ." But again I paused before uttering the thought, before speaking what I did not really want to believe.

"Want to do something for me, Billy?"

"Yes sir!"

"Give the horses a little workout before you turn in. They ain't been rode for a week, any of them. I'm afraid to leave this place any more, even for half an hour. For all we know there's a couple of Government agents right over there in the willows just waiting for a chance like that. They weren't there last night but they might be now. Come on, I'll help you bridle them."

We walked to the corral where the horses still lingered, though the pasture gate hung wide open. The horses were hoping for grain. We gave them each a double handful and bridled them. I didn't bother with a saddle.

First I climbed up on Rocky, the big sorrel stallion —since he was the meanest and fastest I wanted to get that over with quick. As the horse finished his feed I watched the old man walking slowly toward the unlit ranch-house, his dim figure fading into the darkness under the trees. The dogs trotted beside him, whining at his knees, aware that something was wrong.

The big sorrel vibrated under me, snorting with impatience, stamping his foot. I turned him toward the gateway. He broke at once into a lope and I didn't attempt to hold him back. As we cleared the gate he shifted into a full run, head and neck stretching forward.

The wind blew in my face. I hugged him with my knees, twisted my free hand in his mane, and let him go. We raced through the purple gloom straight south toward the fence, over the short tough yellow grass, the stones, the dried-out irrigation channels.

Tears of joy welled from my eyes, drawn out by the wind we were creating. As the dark stretch of the fence swept toward us I was fascinated for a moment by the wild notion of urging the horse over it, over the fence, and heading him toward the mountains and never coming back.

But we both had better sense. At the last instant I laid the rein on the side of his neck and we veered sharply to the right, gouging the sod as we leaned far over. Sparks flashed in the dark as the iron hooves struck on rock.

We ran westward now, toward the broad dim bed of the Salado. Again I was tempted by fantasy: I thought of the yellow eyes, the mystic spring beneath the rock, the lion waiting for us in the hills.

The horse ran eagerly toward that fate, his thousand pounds of muscle and bone and blood and nerve and spirit barely touching the earth, as if our terrific momentum had given us wings. Rolling toward us was the bank of the river, a six-foot jump-off, the broad wash of sand, the grove of trees beyond, the desert and the hills and the mountains beyond that.

But for the second time I resisted the mad idea. We cut right again and galloped upslope back toward the corral and barn, toward the ranch-house and the old man, toward the road that linked us to the world of men and women. And I knew that I would never do what I had dreamed of doing—not in this life.

Three times I raced the splendid horse around the pasture, till I felt him begin to tire. I drew him back to a canter, to a trot, to a walk. We halted close by the corral gate, I slid off, gave the big sorrel a quick rub with the brush, pulled off the bridle, and turned him free with a whack on the shoulder. He sprang away, snorting in triumph. I untied old Blue and climbed on his broad back, my body trembling, my ribs aching with a pleasurable sort of pain, and my brain now free, devoid of all ideas but work.

When I was finished with Blue and the skillet-foot I walked slowly to my room in the bunkhouse. A pleasant fatigue pervaded my bones and flesh and I was ready for sleep again. The sunset by now had dwindled to a single streak of yellow among the stars and the black-blue clouds over the mountains. One of the dogs barked from his place on the ranch-house verandah, scented me out and went silent. The big August frogs clanked along the ditch, strange birds whistled in the depths of the cottonwoods, and an owl—the owl—spoke once from his perch somewhere in the grove by the wash, startling the rabbits and ground squirrels that crept about in the night.

My room seemed stifling and close, though both door

and window were wide open. As I'd done many times before, I dragged the steel cot out of the room into the open and prepared to bed down under the sky. I sat down on the bunk, tugged off my boots, peeled off the socks, and scraped my bare feet in the sand.

I looked toward the ranch-house. One light burned in the kitchen window but I heard no sound. I drew my corncob pipe from its hiding place in the foot of my bedroll, filled it with a cheap harsh workingman's tobacco, lit up and smoked for a while, rubbing my feet on the rough ground.

Despite the birds and frogs, the ranch seemed unnaturally quiet, until I remembered that except for the milk cow and her calf, all our cattle—and half our horses—were gone.

I knocked the ashes from my pipe, hid it away, undressed and slipped into the sack. Hands under my head, I gazed at the sky. The Big Bear hung aloft, steady as rock, with the Pole Star above him.

The world was right. I could close my eyes.

With Cruzita gone, Grandfather had given me the chore of milking the cow. I didn't care for the assignment but the calf was weaned, the job had to be done, even though we had little use for the milk: I wouldn't drink much of it and Grandfather drank none at all.

I washed the cow's udders, set the enameled pail in place and drew the milk while the cow ate the alfalfa in the manger. When I was finished I covered the pail, carried it into the kitchen, and put it in the big refrigerator.

We ate breakfast. The kitchen, with only one window open, was very dark and cool. As we ate we talked about the cow, about the horses, about my escape from the train. We agreed that my suitcase should have reached Pittsburgh by now. What would happen to it there? Neither of us cared. It simply meant that I'd run short on socks and underwear for a while.

After breakfast, as I was washing the dishes and the

old man inspected his shotgun, carbine and revolver for the tenth or twentieth time, we heard the dogs start to bark.

We looked out. Here came the Air Force again, two blue jeeps bristling with yellow helmets and radio antennae. Grandfather slammed shut the kitchen shutters, bolted them, blocked the window with mattress and bedstead, picked up his shotgun and stepped to the open front door with me close behind him.

The jeeps stopped out in the yard under the trees, fifty feet or more from the house. The men got out. Air Police, they were terribly overdressed for the desert summer, with their harness and pistols and badges and boots. Instead of coming toward the house they went to work at once nailing the familiar metal posters to the walls of our outbuildings, the signs in red, white and blue that said "U. S. Government Property—Keep Out." The officer in charge of the project gave us a hard look as we watched from the verandah but said nothing to his men.

Grandfather pulled up his rocking chair and sat down, resting the shotgun across his legs. We watched the police nail their little signs to the hayshed, the bunkhouse, Peralta's house, the stables and even to the tree trunks. Grandfather made no interference.

But when the officer and one of the men, tin placard in hand, came toward us on the porch, the old man stood up, broke open the shotgun, slipped in two fat twelve-gauge cartridges, and closed the breech. The firm clash of the action rang out beautifully through the morning stillness.

The officer and his man stopped, about twenty feet away.

"Sorry, sir," the officer began, after a second of hesitation, "but my orders—"

"Forget your orders!" Grandfather said, softly but clearly. "The first man that touches a hand to my house is going to get a charge of buckshot in the face. And the second charge is for you, Lieutenant." He held the shotgun loosely in his hands, allowing the muzzle to point toward the side and down.

The Air Force continued to pause. Both men, the officer and the sergeant at his side, were sweating richly under their plastic helmets. Sweat darkened the armpits and sides of their khaki shirts.

The officer took another step forward. Grandfather raised the muzzle of the shotgun a few inches, still not pointing it directly at the enemy.

"Mr. Vogelin," the lieutenant said, clearing his throat loudly, "you better think about what you're doing. You're just making a lot more trouble for yourself."

"Let's not talk," Grandfather said. "Please go away before I kill somebody."

The sergeant, big and burly and angry, the sweat glistening on his face, grew impatient. "To hell with all this," he growled, "no old crackpot is gonna stop me." And he stepped toward the house.

Grandfather raised the muzzle of the shotgun and aimed it at the sergeant's face. "Stop."

The sergeant stopped, considering those two black holes that yawned before him.

We waited for a moment.

"Let's go," the lieutenant said, breaking the silence. In the background I noticed the other police watching us. "We'll be back," the lieutenant said to the old man. "Come on, Harry," he said, pulling at the sergeant's sleeve. The sergeant was still glaring at Grandfather across the twin barrels of the shotgun. "I said come on."

"I'm gonna kill this old crank," the sergeant said.

"No you're not. Not today. Let's go." And the lieutenant turned and walked back toward his jeep.

The sergeant spat on the ground, staring Grandfather in the eye, then reluctantly showed his back and retreated to his jeep. Together the two jeeps were driven off through the shade, past the shed and corral and up the slope of the *barranca* into the heat and mirages of the plain.

While Grandfather waited on the porch with the

shotgun, in case the enemy should decide to come back, I took a claw hammer out of the pickup truck and one by one removed all the little red, white and blue signs. All of them.

After that we celebrated our small victory with rum and water and ice. The old man even allowed me a few swallows.

8

All morning we waited for the next attack. It failed
to come. After a dinner of eggs and chili, potatoes and
beans and iced coffee, I went for a ride on Blue while
the old man sat on his rocking chair on the porch, shotgun across his knees and a look of sad resolution on
his face.

That expression frightened me. I was glad to leave
for an hour and wished very much that Lee would
come.

The gelding and I walked along the Salado under the
shelter of the trees. The sun roared directly overhead,
baking the desert in a savage white glare. All was still
except for a number of locusts that screamed continuously from invisible sources in the brush. It was really
much too hot for riding, for work or war, for any form
of physical effort. All living things were shaded up for
the afternoon.

Blue and I did the same. I unbridled him and sat
down against a cottonwood. There was no saddle to
take off since I was in the habit of riding bareback
when staying near the ranch-house. The horse, free,
wandered a few paces away, snuffling at the sunburnt
weeds along the bank. He soon stopped, deep in the
deep green shade of the quiet trees, closed his eyes and
went to sleep, his head drooping, his skin making in-
voluntary twitches under the bites of flies.

The Salado was completely dry. Not a trickle flowed
on the surface of the riverbed; whatever water remained had gone underground several weeks before.

From where I sat, looking across the wash toward the ranch-house, I could see a few of the waterholes which the cattle had dug in the sand, when we still had cattle. These holes were now lined with cakes and shards of baked mud, each fragment curled at the edges and brittle as chinaware.

I sometimes wondered what would happen if the deep well by the house went dry. From that one well came all the water we had at this time of year—for household use, for the horses, for keeping the pasture grass alive. The well out west at the base of the hills would usually produce water, but that was four miles away. There were also a couple of unreliable waterholes farther up the Salado. The only completely dependable source was the spring high in the hills where I'd seen the mountain lion. According to Grandfather that spring had never been known to fail. I supposed that if the drouth got worse we would have to retreat to our mountain cabin.

I looked for rain but the sky was an unflawed blue from horizon to horizon, the beautiful clear blue that promised only heat and thirst and death.

Across the sand, tamarisk and willows, the ranch-house and outbuildings lay on the bench of ground above the river, partially shielded from the direct blast of the sun by the fat old cottonwoods, whose acid-green leaves contrasted strangely with the dun-colored earth, the tawny brush, the iron-red bluffs behind the ranch.

I could see the verandah of the house, where I knew Grandfather was waiting, but the shade in which he sat was so black, so profound, that I could not make out the old man himself, until he stirred, shifting his limbs —then I saw the glint of gun metal. And after that a wisp of smoke, faint and aery as a spirit, floated out of the darkness and I knew he had puffed on his cigar.

In the crystal silence I heard, above the whine of the locusts, the scratching noise of Grandfather's rocking chair on the wooden boards of the porch.

I dozed off but opened my eyes a moment later when I heard the far-off drone of an engine. Looking up, I saw a plume of dust rising beyond the edge of the mesa, which meant that a car was nearing the ranch.

Joyfully I thought of Lee, jumped up and started to run across the riverbed, dragging the bridle reins on the sand. Halfway across I saw the car round the ledge at the top of the rise; it was not Lee's car but a gray government sedan. My heart seemed to drop a few inches. I stopped running.

I waded through the sand and the palpable heat, pushed through the willow and tamarisk thickets on the far side, and walked up over the burnt-over ground to the ranch-house, where Grandfather watched and waited for the uninvited guest.

The car came close and stopped in the shade. One man got out, the only man in the car. It was DeSalius again, smartly dressed in a tan summer suit and a narrow-brimmed hat; under his arm he carried the briefcase.

I reached the house first and took my stand beside the old man, waiting for our visitor.

Spangles of hot light flowed over his hat and shoulders as DeSalius walked toward us under the trees. He had to pass through an area open to the sun and instantly his whole figure paled and seemed to shrink. He entered shade again, coming close, and this made him look plausibly dangerous. But he was smiling his usual pleasant smile, affable as an undertaker, and though he could not help but see the shotgun on Grandfather's lap he came without hesitation right up to the steps of the porch. He paused there, took off his hat and wiped his damp bald head with a handkerchief.

"Mr. Vogelin," he said. "Good afternoon, sir." When the old man made no response to his salute DeSalius looked at me, his bright little blue eyes curiously intent. "What's this I hear about you wrecking a train in El Paso?"

"I didn't wreck any train—sir," I said sullenly.

Colonel DeSalius, mind and eyes wandering, shifted to my grandfather, obviously waiting for an invitation to sit down. But the old man was slow to extend the usual courtesies. To cover his embarrassment, if he was embarrassed, if it was possible for DeSalius to be embarrassed by anything, the visitor spoke again to me. "I read about it in the papers, Billy. All about the boy who pulled the emergency stop and almost wrecked the Southern Pacific's crack train. Wasn't that you?"

I didn't trouble myself to answer.

"What do you want, DeSalius?" Grandfather said.

The colonel smiled, glancing at the chair beside the old man's rocker. "May I sit down?"

"Sit down."

DeSalius took the chair and rearranged it so that he could look at both the old man and the desert to the west. He fanned his red face with the trim straw hat and stared in silence, in unDeSalius-like silence, out into the furnace of the afternoon toward the wash, the trees, the bleached desert, toward Thieves' Mountain floating like a purple ship in the distance,

This was the season of the mirage: if you watched the mountains steadily for more than a few minutes you'd likely see them shift in location and alter in shape, great peaks sliding off their bases and riding on waves of light and heat.

Grandfather puffed on his cigar. DeSalius lit a cigarette. The awful heat made even speech seem difficult.

"Billy," the old man said, "would you fetch us a pitcher of ice water?"

"Yes sir."

I rose from my roost against the wall and moved into the dark interior, The contrast between outside and inside was so great that for a minute I had to feel my way to the kitchen before my eyes adjusted themselves to the darkness.

As I filled a pitcher with water and broke ice cubes from a tray I heard DeSalius begin to speak, discoursing in his rich resonant voice on the weather: the heat, the drouth, the prospects for rain. But I did not hear my grandfather make any reply. How could he? What can the weather mean to a rancher who's been robbed of his vocation? I returned to the porch with ice water and glasses.

"Thank you, Billy."

The ice clinked cheerily in the glasses. We drank. Outside, in the glare, only the locusts seemed to be alive. Something about the terrible heat seemed to drive them into a frenzy of joy—or was it agony? Nothing else moved. Across the wash I could see the outline of old Blue standing with lowered head under the cottonwoods, asleep.

DeSalius sighed comfortably as he lowered his glass and drew on his cigarette. All of us were looking out toward the desert. "You like this country, eh Mr. Vogelin?"

Grandfather stirred. "Like it?"

"Yes. I mean, you like living here."

"This is my home. I was born here. I'm going to die here."

"Yes, I see. That's what I mean." DeSalius paused. There was a tone of wonder in his voice when he went on:

"Don't you ever miss the sight of green grass, Mr. Vogelin? Of running water?—I mean clear steady running water, not these flash floods of liquid mud you have out here. Don't you ever want to live where you're in sight of the homes of other men? Of towns and cities? Of human activity, civilization, great enterprises under way in which whole nations participate?"

"Yes," the old man said, after a moment's reflection, "yes, I miss seeing those things. But not much."

DeSalius smiled. "You're a cynic, Mr. Vogelin." He smoked his cigarette, staring toward Los Ladrones— the mountain of thieves. "You know, I can understand your affection for this desert country. I can't share it but I can understand it, even sympathize with it. This country is—almost sublime. Space and grandeur, a spacious grandeur that's overwhelming. And yet—it isn't quite human, is it? By that I mean it's not really meant for human beings to live in. This is a land for gods, perhaps. Not for men."

"The Apaches liked it," Grandfather said.

"The Apaches? Oh yes, the Apaches. A stone-age people."

"They drive pickup trucks and watch television and drink beer out of tin cans."

"Ah yes," DeSalius said, "quite true. Quite remarkable. Adaptable people. Quite remarkable." He paused. "Mr. Vogelin," he began abruptly, with a brisk transformation of his manner and tone, "we are going to let you stay here."

And for the first time he stopped gazing at the desert and turned his head to watch my grandfather's reaction.

The old man did not reveal any gratitude. "Nobody is going to *let* me stay here," he said, staring back at DeSalius with steady eyes and level gaze.

"Well, I mean we're not going to try to evict you, put it that way, if you prefer. Now understand that I'm talking about the ranch-house only. This does not apply to the land, only to the house and the outbuildings. We're going to allow—we're going to concede your right to retain possession of this house and access to it for the remainder of your natural life. Technically and legally, the house will remain government property, but we are ready to sign an agreement granting you all the rights of ownership except those of sale or transfer. As a matter of fact we've already drawn up the papers."

DeSalius unzipped his handsome cowhide briefcase. "I've got them right in here." He poked his fingers among sheaves of documents—tools of the paper civilization. "There is one condition we must attach to this agreement," He pulled out the paper, complete with carbons and copies, and looked it over, apparently waiting for Grandfather to ask what the attached condition might be.

But the old man did not ask. Shotgun on his lap, cigar in his teeth, he stared out through his spectacles at the mountains, seeming already to have lost interest in the proposition. Or maybe he was uttering a silent prayer of thankfulness—I don't know.

"The further condition," DeSalius continued, after waiting in vain for Grandfather to ask about it, "is that you agree to leave these premises during test periods, that is, on those days when rocket firings will take place." He stopped, watching the old man slyly out of the corners of his eyes. Still no reaction. "I realize this may be an inconvenience but I'm sure you'll agree it's a small price to pay in return for the privilege—for the right of living in your house at all other times. You'll want to go to town occasionally anyway."

As Grandfather still made no answer or revealed any emotion, DeSalius hurried on:

"Now this testing program will become more active over the years. We don't deny that. But it's never likely to exceed, say, seven or eight days a month. Each time a firing is scheduled you will be given a forty-eight hours advance notice. You will never be required to leave this house for more than two or three days at a time, I can almost guarantee that, and if the house is ever damaged, which is highly unlikely—the odds against it are something like a thousand to one—you will be fully compensated, just as you have been compensated for the acquisition of your ranch lands and the auction of your cattle.

"As I may have mentioned, this agreement applies to the adjacent buildings also." DeSalius twirled his hand in the general direction of the sheds, corral, windmill and tank. "They too will be retained in your possession, to use as you see fit. If you wish you are perfectly welcome to keep a few horses on the place. The Government would have no objection to that, although we could not assume responsibility for their safety during test periods. As I said, our only stipulation is that you agree to leave the premises and the test area when a rocket firing is scheduled. In return for this minor concession the Government concedes to you the right to possess, live in and, as I said, enjoy the benefits of your family home for the remainder of your natural life, which, judging by your appearance, sir, should be for many years indeed."

DeSalius finally stopped talking. You could see the effort it cost him—to stop talking. With firm resolution he shut his face for a minute and waited for a response from my grandfather.

But there was no response. The old man continued to gaze toward the mountains, his face calm, his hands still.

DeSalius waited, wiped the sweat from his brow and bald scalp, puffed on his cigarette, took a quick look at the mountains himself, rubbed his knee and rattled the papers in his hand. Finally, unable to wait any longer, he took a pen from his coat pocket and offered it, together with the papers, to the old man. "Well, sir, if you'll sign this agreement now—there at the bottom, I've marked the place—we can conclude this discussion."

The old man made no move. Hands reposed on the stock of the shotgun, he looked out over the desert toward the hills.

"Well, sir?" DeSalius said, holding pen and papers in the air.

At last the old man spoke. "No," he said.

"Beg your pardon?"

"No."

DeSalius very slowly withdrew his extended hands, putting the pen back in his coat pocket and the documents back in the briefcase. He left the briefcase open, however. Taking the new straw hat, which had been perched on one knee, the colonel fanned his heated face with one hand and poured himself another glassful of ice water with the other hand.

The ice jingled merrily, musically, as the chill water burbled through the spout of the pitcher. The pitcher was covered with a cold dew. When DeSalius finished pouring I reached for the pitcher myself.

"Sir, this is absolutely our final offer," DeSalius said, sounding like a pitchman for a used-car lot.

"No," said my grandfather. His favorite word.

"Absolutely your last opportunity." The colonel took a deep drink of water, cooling his mouth and throat and gut. I could feel another speech coming.

It came: "The Government has been very patient with you, Mr. Vogelin, very patient and very generous. Extremely generous. Though we easily could, we have not yet proceeded to take advantage of the fact that your intransigence constitutes not only a violation of the law but also, in this case, a *willful* and *deliberate obstruction* of the national defense effort. You, sir, are the only man in this entire area who has not been able to see that national security takes precedence over private property and private sentiments. Are you aware of that Mr. Vogelin?"

Grandfather did not reply.

DeSalius went on:

"All of your neighbors have long since conceded this point and have allowed the Government to proceed with its necessary functions, meaning, in this regard, the provision for the national defense and the security of all Americans, including, Mr. Vogelin, yourself. The Government has no concern more vital in these times than the protection of all of us, our families and ourselves, against the menace, the ever-present menace, if I may say so, of a Soviet attack."

The pause. The silence. I sipped my ice water, listening and observing with every nerve.

"Now Mr. Vogelin," DeSalius said, "you have had almost six months, sir, *six months* . . . to reflect on this matter. You have been most generously compensated in every way. Furthermore you have been treated courteously, patiently, and fairly, with an indulgence for your stubbornness that exceeds all precedent. You have abused and threatened our officers and we

have taken no legal action in reprisal. You have tres-
passed against Government property and we have
chosen to disregard that. You have ignored and defied
three court orders and we have even allowed that to
pass. No other nation on earth, except one as great and
powerful and humane as ours, could tolerate such insolent violations of legality. But Mr. Vogelin—"
DeSalius stared earnestly at the old man "Mr. Vogelin, the time has come when this Government must act.
This Government can no longer wait upon your pride
and obstinacy. We have made this final generous offer,
allowing you to live here subject only to the certain
conditions I have mentioned. Now Mr. Vogelin, in the
light of what I have said, I ask you to reconsider your
decision. Will you accept our offer?"

Grandfather reconsidered. For about a minute. "I'm
sure grateful for all you people have done for me." He
stopped at that.

"And about the offer?" DeSalius insisted.

"The offer. Yes, the offer." The old man spoke
softly and slowly. "Yes, Colonel, that's a damn generous offer," He stopped again.

DeSalius reached toward his pen and briefcase.
"Then you accept?"

"No."

"Mr. Vogelin, you must be reasonable. This is your
last chance."

"You said that before."

"Sir, we're not bluffing now, we're not bluffing. We
mean business. That you must understand."

"Don't fret, DeSalius, I believe you."

"Will you reconsider?"

"No."

DeSalius lapsed into stillness. He stared at the floor.
The concavity of his chest, the slump of his shoulders,
suggested a man driven beyond mere exasperation.
"Mr. Vogelin," he said, speaking slowly and quietly to
the floor, "we have done everything we could to spare
you embarrassment, to compensate you fully, to allow

you plenty of time, to help you under stand why this removal is necessary. You have refused to cooperate. Mr. Vogelin, we cannot permit you to defy the Court any longer. If you refuse this final offer, sir, the Government will have no recourse but to fall back upon the direct instruments of the law."

"Direct instruments? That sounds like what I've been expecting," the old man said. "You mean that marshal, I suppose. You better tell him, DeSalius, to bring plenty of help when he comes. He'll need it"

"He will get all that he needs, sir. And I must warn you that not only will you be evicted by force, if necessary, but you will also be subject to such charges as contempt of court, resisting an officer of the law and trespassing on Government property. You must realize what that can mean. You're rather old for prison life, sir, if I may say so."

The old man smiled. "Don't bother trying to scare me, Colonel. I'm too old for that too. No sir, we'll settle the whole business right here under the trees. Send your marshal around. I'm ready."

Again DeSalius fell silent, staring out of the verandah shade toward the awful brute glare of the desert. Far off on the shimmering waves of heat and light Thieves' Mountain drifted to the north, fifty miles, apparently, from its usual anchorage.

"You know, Mr. Vogelin," DeSalius said after a while, "this will be the first time in my career as a trial attorney for the Corps of Engineers that I will have had to resort to force to carry out legal procedures. Unless you change your mind. The first time in over fifteen years."

"I'm sorry to hear that."

DeSalius shifted about in his chair. He finished his glass of ice water and put his hat on, picked up his briefcase and stood up. He held out his right hand to Grandfather; Grandfather ignored the gesture.

"I want to thank you for your hospitality, Mr. Vogelin. You've been kind. Thank you, Billy, for the ice

water, which was a great relief on a day like this. Sir,"
he went on, addressing Grandfather, "I'll see you
again soon. Very soon. And under somewhat different
conditions."

"How soon?" Grandfather asked.

"I'm not prepared to reveal that, sir. But it will be
soon. Very soon indeed. Perhaps within a few days.
Perhaps within a few hours. The Government is going
to take steps, sir, that you will be able to understand."

"About time," Grandfather said, not in mockery of
the man but in genuine relief.

Suddenly DeSalius seemed on the verge of losing his
temper. Maybe the heat was getting him. "Sir, don't
you—" he burst out, but he halted himself at once.

He turned sullenly away from us, stepped off the
porch and out into the naked blaze of the sun, where
his skin and straw hat withered perceptibly.

"Good God, this is a horrible place," we heard him
say, as he walked toward his car. He sounded half-
delirious, muttering to himself as he shambled through
the dust. I nearly pitied him—his beautiful new suit
rumpled and stained with sweat, his hat wilting, his
sharp shoes coated with dust, his shoulders rounded in
defeat.

But when he reached the car, before getting in, he
faced us with his old fake smile. "Goodbye, Mr. Vogelin. I've really enjoyed our little conversation. Goodbye, Billy. Be a good boy, help your grandfather all
you can. See you again."

He climbed with difficulty into the low-slung car,
started the motor and drove violently away, sweeping
in a wide U-turn around our pickup, under the trees
and up the road past corral and barn and sheds toward
the bluffs of clay that gleamed like fired iron under the
sun.

When he was out of sight Grandfather and I stared
at each other without speaking a word.

In the evening after supper came Lee Mackie with our mail, with fresh provisions, with news and advice and good cheer.

We celebrated—something. The rum gurgled from the gallon jug. The ice tinkled in the glasses. When the old man wasn't looking, I sneaked some rum into my Coke, lacing it good.

We sat on the verandah and watched the spectacular death of a day in the sky beyond the mountain range: cloudy islands of auburn, purple and whisky-tinted snow, swan-necked birds with fiery wings as long as the mountains, golden lakes, seas of silver and green. Nighthawks plunged for supper in the foreground, black darts against the radiant light, the wind roaring through their wings. Bats flickered here and there, the horned owl sounded from his tree across the wash, and the horses stamped and shuffled at the water trough in the corral. From the mountains miles away came another sound which only I could hear—the scream of the lion.

"Now old horse, he's right: it's a fair offer; you should take it. It's your last chance."

Lee clutched his drink with his right hand and beat on the arm of his chair with the left. "Yes, John, you're a fool to turn this down. Can't you see it's a victory for you? They're giving in. They never made a deal like this with anyone else. You got 'em buffaloed, you old buzzard. If you turn this deal down, why I won't know what to think. About you. Why I might begin to think you're turning into a . . . a wild-eyed fanatic. Yeah, that's the word, a fanatic. Would anything like this happen in Russia? Why they'd simply put a bullet through your neck. My God, John, you can't expect the whole United States Government to give in to you completely. They've got face to save too."

He stopped for a drink.

Grandfather, silent and unsmiling, highball in hand and the shotgun still on his lap, made no reply but continued to stare darkly into the west.

I saw a scorpion, stinger aloft, race across the boards and slip into a black crack.

Lee poured <u>himself</u> a fresh drink and rambled on, his face glowing with good humor and good intentions, his eyes bright with alcohol:

"I've talked this over with Annie, John, and she feels the same way I do. That this is a great offer, the best you'll ever get, and you should accept it. In fact everybody in town has heard about it by now, don't ask me how but you know how the word gets around, and they all think you're a fool for turning it down. A fool —or something worse. I tell you, there's not a man in New Mexico could agree with you now. If you reject this deal why there won't be any sympathy for you at all any more. None at all."

"I think Grandfather is right," I said.

"You hush up," Lee said, smiling briefly.

"Billy's still with me," Grandfather said. "You're still with me, Lee."

"That's right, of course, we're still with you. You can count on that. But my God—"

"As long as you two are with me I don't care what the rest of the world thinks."

"All right," Lee said, "that makes three of us." He drank, wiped his mouth on the back of his hand and confronted us with his handsome, eager dark face. "Three of us against the whole United States Government and about a hundred and eighty million other Americans."

"Three's enough," the old man said. "Might even be . . . too many. What do they say about three?"

"Now don't talk that way. What do you mean?" Lee did not wait for an answer but rushed onward. "John, what more do you want? They'll let you keep your house. You got that sixty-five thousand-dollar check waiting for you at District Court. Enough for a down payment on lots of far better cattle outfits than this ever was or ever could be."

"I wouldn't touch their money with a shovel."

"You ought to think of other people, old horse. Think of your daughters. They could sure use some of that money. Think of the boy here. You could set him up good with a wad like that."

"I wouldn't touch it either," I said.

"You keep out of this," Grandfather said. Gently.

"Yes sir." I sipped on my rum Coke.

"Listen, John," Lee said, "I wonder if it ever occurred to you that you might be acting kind of selfish about all this. For the sake of some mysterious kind of —point of honor, you are losing your home, depriving your kin of considerable benefits, and maybe risking your own liberty. Because you know damn well if you keep this up you're going to wind up in jail. In a Federal prison. Maybe worse, if you shoot some poor soldier boy who's only trying to do his duty. Did you ever think of that?"

"I've thought of it."

"Well think about it some more. And think hard. You don't have much time left. Maybe only a few days."

"Maybe only a few hours," I volunteered.

Lee looked at me. "Why don't you go for a ride, shorty? Those horses need some work." His white smile shone through the twilight; that mouthful of perfect teeth.

"Will you go with me?"

He hesitated. The smile weakened, returned. "Yes! Let's go. Right now." He emptied his glass and jumped up. "Come on, Billy, we'll have a race."

"I'll race you," I said, feeling high and glorious myself. I finished my drink and stood up.

"You two be careful," the old man said. "Don't pitch into some gopher hole in the dark and break your fool necks. Think of the horses."

"We'll think of the horses, John. You think of Billy and your daughters. Come on, Billy."

I jumped off the porch and started at a run toward the corral. Lee came running after and caught me halfway. Putting his arm around my shoulders he slowed me to a walk. He was panting a little. "Now you listen to me." Panting. "Billy, you listen. You have some influence over your crazy grandfather. Right? He loves you. He might listen to what you say. You understand?"

I nodded.

"All right. You should try to use this influence you have—in a sensible way. Don't keep on encouraging the old man. You understand? Try to make him listen to reason. You understand me?"

"No." I said. "No I don't, Lee."

"What's the use—you're just like him."

We reached the corral, climbed through, and bridled old Blue and Grandfather's big sorrel. Skilletfoot as usual would be left out. I threw myself up on Blue's back and struggled to a sitting position, clutching the mane. Lee vaulted onto the back of the stallion.

"Go ahead, Billy. I'll give you a ten-second start."

"Where we going?"

"Twice around the pasture. Close to the corners. Go ahead. One—two—"

I kicked Blue with my heels and he leaped forward, through the open gateway of the corral and into the field of twilight. At a dead run I bore straight for the southeast corner, counting to myself. When I reached the number eleven I heard a wild whoop from Lee and knew he'd started.

Reins loose in my right hand, left hand twisting the wiry hairs of the mane, I beat my heels on Blue's flanks and watched the fence come toward us. At the corner we pivoted sharply and raced toward the southwest. In my rear I heard the sod-muted thunder of the stallion's hooves.

"Let's go, Blue," I shouted, my body forward over his neck, my chin between his ears. The wind rushed by, the gloom parted wonderfully before us, I felt the beating of my mount's great heart between my knees, the surge of his muscles under my body.

The corner rose before us, we turned and galloped

north, along the fence and the ledge of the river. Iron clashed on stone, sparks flashed in the velvet air. "Come on, Blue, come on," I panted in his ear. But old Blue was doing his best already; there was no further response. Sucking wind like a steam engine, he neared the northwest corner, swung right and galloped heavily upslope toward the ranch buildings. Halfway there Lee came alongside on the slick-gaited Rocky and bellowed at me:

"Shag him, Billy!"

The sorrel flowed steadily past us in a gleam of sweat and silken strength, pulled ahead, and created a gap which grew wider at every pace. When we turned at the northeast corner by the corral Lee was three lengths ahead and old Blue was beginning to falter. We were licked but he kept on running. I couldn't have stopped him if I'd tried.

Lee was waiting for me inside the corral, brushing his horse, when Blue and I trotted in.

I slid off, removed the bridle and sloughed the gobs of lather off Blue's trembling shoulders and chest. "Some race," I said in disgust.

"Old Blue did pretty good," Lee said. "He's a big-hearted old brute. Here." He gave me the brush.

"Next time I'll ride the stud," I said.

"Why sure, Billy. And we'll hang a sack of grain under his belly. And you'll give me a bigger start."

"Yeah, sure."

"You did pretty good. Don't get mad."

"I'll race you back to the house," I said. "On foot."

"You win already. Let's walk."

We gave the horses each a double handful of grain, turned them loose and walked back to the ranch-house, toward the red glow of the old man's cigar. Again Lee tried to sweet-talk me into compromise. Arm over my shoulders, he said,

"Billy, old buddy, I want you to do me a favor. Will you do me a favor?"

"Sure. Anything."

"Talk to your grandfather. Tell him not to go on with his crazy idea. Tell him to use his head."

I was silent.

"Will you, Billy? It's for his own good. You don't want the old man to get shot, do you? Or locked up in prison for the rest of his life?"

"No."

"Fine. Now we're getting somewhere. Will you ask him to take DeSalius up on that last offer?"

I hesitated.

"Will you?"

"No."

"My God, you sound just like the old man."

"I think he's in the right, Lee. Don't you?"

After a moment Lee said, "I don't really know, Billy. To tell the truth I don't really know."

"You're going to help him, aren't you?"

The tall man squeezed my arm. "Don't worry about that. That's one thing you don't have to worry about."

Gratefully I smiled up at Lee.

"Who won?" the old man shouted as we approached the house. The owl behind the wash echoed his call.

"We did," Lee answered, hugging me close.

"Lee won," I explained as we climbed the porch steps, "But he was riding Rocky."

We sat beside the old man and listened to the owl. The darkness was settling in fast, the lights fading over the mountains and the stars emerging, one by one, from the violet sky.

After some talk about the horses, the dry spell and the falling water table, Lee and Grandfather returned to the subject of real interest. This time Lee pursued it farther and with a greater intensity than ever before, as if with the knowledge that this might be the final opportunity to drive a wedge of logic and sense into the old man's bitter mind.

"It's not only the practical side of the thing," Lee was saying, as I half-dozed, half-listened nearby, "you also have to think about the question of justice. Now you never before reared up on your hind legs and defied the law, the country and the Constitution. As long as you weren't personally affected by what was going on, you seemed to consent to the laws and customs and so on. Many other people have to go through what's happening to you, John, and you never protested against it before."

"They have their choice," the old man said.

"All right. It's easy to say that now. But maybe the Government is really in the right here. If they need your land for the sake of the national security shouldn't you give it up? Which is more important, your property or the national safety?"

"Nobody's safe when the Government can take away his home."

"Nobody would be safe in a world run by the Soviet Union."

"All right," Grandfather said, "there's no safety anywhere. I don't want safety. I want to die on my father's ranch." Grandfather puffed on his cigar: the red coal flared and faded, casting a dim transient light over the tough features of his face.

I smuggled more rum into my soda pop.

"Sometimes we have to make a choice between evils," Lee said. "Maybe in a case like this military necessity is more important than your private desires. Am I right or wrong?"

"Wrong," I said, lifting my glass.

"You be quiet, child," the old man said to me. Quietly. To Lee he said, "I can see the sense in your argument. Not much but some. But all my feelings go against it. This is my home. I was born here. My father worked and fought all his life for this place. He died here. My mother died here. My wife almost died here. Now I want to die here, when I'm ready to die. I will not live here part-time as some sort of charity ward of the Government, while they think up new ways to wedge me off completely. No, by God, I can't do that. I'll fight it out with bullets before I'll do that."

Lee was silent for a while, as he stared with his good earnest eyes at the old man, at the floor, at me, at the old man again. "I know how you feel. I share that feeling. Didn't I spend ten years of my own life on this place? But look, John—" He made a vague gesture with his hand. "Does the land really belong to you? Is it really yours? Does the land belong to anybody? A hundred years ago the Apaches had it, it was all theirs. Your father and other men like him stole it from the Apaches. The railroad company and the big cattle companies and the banks tried to steal it from your father and from you. Now the Government is going to steal it from you. This land has always been crawling with thieves. How do you suppose that mountain over there got its name? A hundred years from now, when we're all dead and buried and forgotten, the land will still be here, will still be the same worthless dried-out burnt-up parcel of sand and cactus it is now. And some other fool of a thief will be stringing a fence around it and hollering that he owns it, that it belongs to him, and telling everybody else to keep out."

Grandfather smiled and drew on the cigar. "I hope his name is Vogelin. Or Starr."

"Why don't you give in, old horse? Give in gracefully, like a gentleman, and let the generals make fools of themselves here for a while. Let them have their turn."

"Let them. I'm willing. But I ain't going to give in like a gentleman. If I have to give in I'm going to give in like an Apache. That's part of the pattern, Lee. That's the tradition around here."

Lee stared hard at Grandfather before breaking into a smile. "You stone-headed old idiot. You *are* crazy. You must be crazy. Hand me that jug."

"Billy, will you get us some more ice?" Grandfather asked.

"Yes sir." I got up from the floor. The wall yawed toward me. I placed a hand on it to hold it up. "Ice," I said.

"Now," Lee said, after a deep sigh, "let's begin all

over again. Let's see if we can't study this thing from some other angle. ...."

"Keep trying," I heard the old man say, as I staggered into the darkness of the kitchen, feeling my way toward the lamp on the table. But the first thing I felt on the table was not the lamp but the rifle and beside it the box of ammunition. I sagged against the table, leaning on it with both hands, and waited for my head to stop swimming.

Through the fog which enclosed me I heard, out in the night, the great horned owl crying for hunger. And in the brush and sand along the wash all the little animals, the rabbits and bannertail mice and ground squirrels, would be listening, frozen in terror.

9

I slept badly that night. Halfway through the night the nausea in my belly became unendurable. I crawled feebly from my bunk, wobbled to the doorway and vomited about a quart of rum, Coke, and half-digested supper onto the ground.

I felt so weak and foul and hopeless that I sank to my hands and knees, fingering my throat and trying to heave up my horrible stomach. Finally, emptied and exhausted, I crept back to bed and fell into uneasy sleep, with dreams of trouble and fear, barking guns and barbed wire, a ripped-open horse and a barren well, clashing through my mind.

The glare of day had returned and my bunkhouse room was full of a stifling heat when I woke up. My head throbbed like a drum, my mouth tasted of filth. I lay on my back for a long time staring at the cobwebs on the ceiling and the circling flies. When the heat became at last too much to take, I sat up and pulled on my jeans, shirt and boots, put on my hat and stumbled outside into the dazzle of daylight. Bearing toward the ranch-house, I tramped dizzily over the stones and weeds, aware of a dark thirst. The sun was high in the east, near eight o'clock, flaming dully through layer upon layer of dust and heat. Lee's car was gone.

Approaching the house I saw Grandfather coming out of the cowpen with the milk pail in hand. He'd let me sleep through my morning chore and faintly ashamed, I mumbled my good morning without looking him in the face.

We entered the house and the kitchen, where the old man put the milk in the refrigerator. I found a cold breakfast of slab bacon and scrambled eggs waiting for me. I didn't want to eat but it seemed necessary: we might be in for a busy day. I forced the greasy stuff into my mouth, chewed without pleasure and swallowed it down, somehow. Coffee seemed to help. I poured a second cupful.

"Billy, you're going home tonight."

"What?" His words came to me through a haze of dizziness and fatigue. "Going home?"

"Tonight." Grandfather held an open letter in his hand. "This is from your mother. Lee brought it last night. She says if I don't send you home within a week she's flying out here to get you. She's mad at me. Lee'll take you down to El Paso again this evening. And this time we're putting you on an airplane. Let's see you try and stop an airplane."

I could do that, too, I thought, if I wanted to. Aloud I said, "But you said I could stay another week, Grandfather."

"That was the day before yesterday. Anyhow, we got these orders from your mother."

I'd been expecting such an ultimatum to arrive. Besides, I was too sick and tired to protest anymore. With dull nerves and a heavy heart I finished my breakfast and washed the dishes.

As for the old man, he walked once more all through the house, inspecting the fortifications, preparing food and water supplies, checking the guns, counting the ammunition. He seemed to me more resolute, less agitated, than ever before. He came back to the kitchen and stood and watched me, polishing his glasses.

"You'd make a good partner, Billy. I'm sorry you have to go."

I said nothing. I felt too resigned and at the same time too bitter to make an argument.

As we stood there in the gloom of the kitchen we heard the rumble of engines, not one but several and approaching rapidly. We went to the front door and looked out. Over the rim of the bluff behind the ranch rose billows of dust,

"Here they come at last," Grandfather said, though as yet we could see nothing but the dust cloud. The first thing he did was put his glasses on. The second thing he did was pick up the shotgun.

"Maybe it's Lee," I said, but the old man shook his head.

The lead government car approached around the turn, came down the winding road and toward the house past the outbuildings and under the trees. The first car was followed by two others, gray government sedans loaded with armed men.

The first car stopped out in the yard, half in the shade. While the driver stayed at the wheel the man beside him got out. It was Burr, the U.S. Marshal. He wore a suit, like DeSalius, like a businessman, and was not armed. But we could see the glint of rifles in the other two cars and the sheen of leather straps and badges. Two men in the first car, counting the marshal, and three in each of the others.

The marshal walked toward us. He was not smiling at all this time.

"Billy," Grandfather whispered to me, "you sneak out to the pickup and get the revolver."

"Yes sir."

I sidled off to the end of the porch while Grandfather, holding his shotgun, waited for the marshal to speak. There was no way for me to get to the pickup truck unobserved; the men in the cars were watching me. So I simply walked as casually as I could toward the truck, hoping no one would pay me any attention. As I went I heard the opening parley between the old man and the marshal.

"Good morning, Mr. Vogelin."

"Stop right there. Stop. Don't come any closer."

"I said good morning, Mr. Vogelin."

"I heard you, Marshal. Now you stop right where you are and don't come one step closer."

"Okay, I'm stopped."

"Stay there."

I looked back. The marshal stood some thirty feet away from the porch steps, full in the harsh glare of the sun and facing the double-barreled shotgun aimed at him from the shadow on the porch.

"Now Mr. Vogelin, I guess you know why I'm here."

"It won't do you any good, Marshal."

"I'm here to help you move, Mr. Vogelin. I'm here to carry out the orders of the Court. Are you ready to leave?"

"I'm not leaving."

"All right, Mr. Vogelin. But I thought I'd give you one last chance to leave peacefully. I'll use force if I have to."

"You'll have to. I'm ready. I'm ready, Marshal. Tell your men to start shooting."

"We don't want anything like that. For godsake listen to reason."

"I've got all the reason I need, Marshal."

I reached the truck, opened the door and half entered, leaning toward the dashboard compartment. But when I opened it I found the revolver gone. I knew I hadn't taken it. Maybe Grandfather—

"Watcha doing, sonny?" One of the marshal's deputies stood behind me, hand on the butt of his pistol. His belt was studded with brass shells.

I decided to make a dash for the house. But before I could get clear of the truck the man grabbed me, twisted my arm behind my back and forced me away from the truck toward the three cars.

"We better keep you out of the way, sonny," the deputy said. "We don't want any children to get hurt."

"You're hurting my arm," I howled.

"I'm sorry." The man eased up a bit on the pressure. As he did so I made another attempt to break free. He tightened his grip again. "Say, don't try that, kid. Take it easy or I'll have to put the cuffs on you."

He pushed me into the back seat of the second car and got in beside me, breathing hard and stinking of sweat. His harness creaked. He looked like a draft horse. The two men in front, also armed and in uniform, ignored us. They were watching and listening to the scene by the verandah, where my grandfather and the marshal were still talking. We had no trouble at all in hearing everything that was said.

"No," the old man was saying, "if you want to get me out of here you'll have to dig me out."

"We'll do that, Mr. Vogelin, if we have to. If you want it that way that's what we'll do. But I ask you, for the last time, don't give us any trouble. Somebody might get bad hurt. Maybe you. Maybe one of us. Maybe me. Somebody might even get killed, Mr. Vogelin. I ask you to think about that. Is it worth it?"

Grandfather answered from the shadows of the porch. In the deep shade we could see little of him, only the dull shine of the shotgun and the twinkle of his glasses.

"You take yourself and your pistol whackers off my property and nobody'll get hurt."

"Can't do that, Mr. Vogelin. These here orders—"

"I don't care what your orders are. I'll kill the first man who sets a foot on this porch or touches a hand to my house."

"Now wait a minute, Mr. Vogelin. Let's talk about this some more."

"There's nothing to talk about. Nothing at all. Either you and your men go away or we shoot it out, that's all. I'm an old man now, I'd as soon die today as any other. It's a nice day. Watch out there, don't try to creep any closer!"

The marshal made a futile gesture with his hands, staring at the specter on the porch. He pushed back his hat and scratched his head. He looked around at me and the seven deputies sitting in the cars. He looked over at the barn and up at the windmill, which was still. He looked up, briefly, at the sun. Ten o'clock. He pulled a watch from his suit and looked at it.

"Well, Mr. Vogelin. . . ." A short plump official with a baggy seat to his trousers, the marshal looked harmless as a mailman. "Well, Mr. Vogelin, I don't know what else I can say. My orders are to get you out of here."

Grandfather made no reply. He waited.

The men in the car with me stared intently toward the house. I reached cautiously for the door handle at my side, found it, pushed down. The latch clicked open. I pushed the door open and rolled out while the deputy reached after me with clawing fingers.

"Grandfather!" I screamed. "Wait for me!"

The deputy caught me by my belt and yanked me back into the car. I fought with him, kicking and punching, until he again grabbed my wrist and bent my arm behind my back.

He held a pair of handcuffs before my eyes. "See these, boy? You see these things? If you don't sit still like a good boy I'm going to put these on you and you won't like that one little bit, no sir."

I relaxed and tried hard not to cry. What hurt me most was not the twisted arm but the realization, the gradual realization that Grandfather had tricked me into leaving the house, that he had sent me after the revolver knowing it was not in the truck and also knowing that I would be captured. I felt betrayed. My nose was running and my eyes threatening to leak. I sniffed.

"Don't cry, sonny," the deputy said, relaxing his grip on my wrist. "You're all right."

"You shut up!" I bawled. "Get your dirty paw off me."

"You're a wild one, ain't you?"

"Here comes Burr," one of the deputies in the front seat said. "Looks like we'll have some fun."

I sat still and looked with the others. The marshal was walking slowly toward us, head bowed and hands in his pockets. The door of the ranch-house slammed shut behind him.

He stopped close to the cars. "Everybody out. Bring your grenades. Stick them on your rifles. Spread out. Take cover. Take the boy out of the firing line."

He stood quietly, not watching, as the men scrambled out of the cars and followed his orders. The man who had captured me pulled me out of the car and led me toward the bunkhouse. Holding my arm in his and gripping my wrist with his huge hand, we stood against the shaded wall and watched the others.

The marshal's men, crouching behind the trees and the outbuildings, were attaching the tear gas grenades to their rifles. I looked toward the house. The verandah was empty now, the door bolted, the last window closed and shuttered; the place looked solid as a fort. I knew that Grandfather was watching through the little gunport he had drilled through the wall halfway between the kitchen window and the front door — watching everything across the sights of his gun.

The marshal, standing in an exposed position near his automobile, studied the situation. With all the doors of the house barred and all the windows shuttered, locked from the inside, his primary problem was how to get the tear gas inside the building.

I watched him speaking to his assistant, saw the assistant speak to one of the deputies, saw the deputy, with several tear gas grenades in his hands, start off in a wide circle around the house toward the bluff in the rear.

But that wouldn't do them any good. In the first place Grandfather would see through the maneuver. In the second place they'd still have to get a man close in to the house to pry open a shutter or climb to the roof. That meant risking somebody's life.

But then I realized that the old man, alone inside, could not possibly cover all the ground surrounding the house. He could not be in two places at the same time. All that the marshal had to do to insure success was send his men up to the house from opposite sides. Even then, however, Grandfather would be able to kill some of them. The marshal was understandably reluctant to risk anyone's life in this operation and he kept us all waiting for a long time, perhaps twenty minutes or more, before he did anything at all other than send the one deputy to the high ground in the rear of the house.

At last he was ready. The marshal stepped out into the scalding sunlight and took a few slow paces toward the house.

"All right, Vogelin," he said loudly, "we're not waiting any more. You ready to come out?"

We all stared toward the house. There was no reply. The marshal turned to one of the deputies near the parked cars. "Give me the ax."

The deputy found an ax in one of the cars and carried it out to the marshal, then returned to his place behind the trunk of a cottonwood.

Holding the ax in his hands, the marshal faced the house. "You see this here ax, Mr. Vogelin? Now I'm coming up there and I'm gonna chop down your front door." He paused. "You hear me, Mr. Vogelin?"

We waited for the answer. There was no answer.

I thought of the old man crouching inside the darkened house, moving from peephole to peephole, front and rear, trying to see everything that was happening. His fort was also a trap. He needed help. He needed me. He needed Lee Mackie.

The marshal took a step toward the house, brandishing the ax. "Here I come Mr. Vogelin," he shouted, loud and clear. "Can you see me? I'm coming to chop down your front door and help you out of there." As he shouted, the marshal took two more deliberate steps toward the house.

Now the man in the rear of the house advanced a little, moving from rock to rock, keeping low and under cover. If he was able to reach the house he might climb to the roof and simply drop the tear gas bombs down the chimneys.

"Grandfather," I yelled, "watch out for the man in "

The deputy's fat hand clapped across my mouth. He screwed my arm behind my back. "You shut up, boy," he said firmly.

"Here I come, Mr. Vogelin," the marshal shouted, taking another step toward the house. "Here I come, look at me."

Something whistled through the air above the marshal's head as we heard the crack of a rifle from the inside of the house.

With amazing alacrity the marshal jumped back and ran for the shelter of the nearest car. At the same time the man in the rear of the house ran forward, reaching the comparative safety of the walls, and began edging his way around a corner toward the nearest of the porch pillars. Climbing that he could attain the roof. But again he might expose himself. So hugging the wall, the deputy waited for the marshal to do something, to give him another chance.

Mr. Burr was slow to act. He was in no hurry to draw the old man's fire again. But something had to be done. The sun was creeping higher, the day was becoming impossibly hot and cruel and exasperating.

We waited, we waited, while the marshal, squatting behind his automobile, consulted with his assistant and one of the deputies. Another five, ten, fifteen minutes passed in this way, with nothing of any apparent importance happening. I knew the time involved because I could read the watch on the hairy wrist of the deputy whose hand was hovering near my mouth.

Where, I wondered, where in God's name was Lee? Now when we needed him more than ever before, he was not here.

At last the marshal prepared to act again. Remaining in the shelter of the car, I heard him call to his men:

"Smoke him out, boys."

Almost simultaneously five rifles went off and five heavy grenades lobbed through the air and crashed against the front of the house, around the doors and windows of the porch. They exploded on contact, releasing billows of yellow gas that gathered under the porch roof, lazily oozing over the edges. Some of the tear gas no doubt seeped into the house through the cracks in the barricaded openings.

I'd almost forgotten the man in the rear. When I looked for him I found him already on the roof of the house crawling toward the nearest of the two chimneys, the one for the living room fireplace. I imagined the bombs bursting in the fireplace and in the kitchen stove, filling the house with their intolerable fumes.

"Grandfather!" I howled, once, before the heavy hand jammed my mouth.

"I'm gonna gag you, sonny," the deputy said, "if you make one more squeak."

There was nothing I could do. In helpless outrage I saw the man on the roof kneel beside the fireplace chimney, cock a grenade and drop it down inside. Dust, gas and smoke flashed up out of the stack as the man moved to the other chimney.

Now the marshal stood up behind his car, scanning the house with anxious eyes, waiting for the front door to fly open and the old man to come stumbling out with his hands on his eyes. But he didn't—not my grandfather.

The deputy on the roof dropped in the rest of his tear gas shells, four in all, and sat down to wait. His position on the roof, though exposed to the sun, was perfectly safe.

As threads of gas leaked out of the house the marshal walked out into the open again and shouted at my grandfather:

"Mr. Vogelin! You better come on out now, Mr. Vogelin. Don't try to breathe that stuff, it might kill you if you breathe too much. Just put a rag over your face and open the front door. Come on out now, Mr. Vogelin, we won't shoot. Everything will be all right."

The door did not open. There was no sound from within the house. Maybe the old man had been able to keep out most of the gas by simply closing the dampers in the chimneys.

The marshal waited a little longer, then stepped forward, once, twice, toward the house, the ax in his hand. He stopped and called again:

"We're waiting for you, Mr. Vogelin. Please come out now. You'll get mighty sick if you don't come out of there, Mr. Vogelin. That gas can make you mighty sick, sometimes too much of it will kill a man. You hear me, Mr. Vogelin?"

Still no reply. The marshal scratched his head, looking around, looking at us, his face grim, shining with sweat. He faced the house, sighed profoundly—I saw his chest rise and fall—and took another step toward the verandah.

Exactly as before, a rifle went off inside the house and the bullet burned through the air close above the marshal's head, plowing through the foliage of the trees.

I watched two leaves fall slowly to the ground. Before they had spanned the distance from the bough to ground the marshal had scurried back to cover and was again in consultation with his assistant, behind the automobile.

And again we waited. Five minutes. Ten minutes. While the sun crawled toward the zenith, flaring horribly, roasting the earth and baking skulls. I felt sorry for the man on the roof, devoid of shade and afraid to try to get down. No, I didn't feel sorry for that dirty scum at all, not when I thought of my grandfather, of the old man waiting inside the house, peering down across the sights of a gun barrel, looking out from his suffocating darkness—if he was still alive—at the blaze of light beating down like golden hail on the world outside. He would see the motionless machines, the tired men crouching in the shade, the continuous shaking of the cottonwood leaves, and across the wash the burnt desert, under layers of undulant heat waves, stretching away for mile after mile toward the beloved and lost, the unattainable mountains.

I felt the deputy relaxing at my side, his breathing slow and deep. Suddenly I broke loose and ran across the open ground toward the house.

"Stop that boy!"

Two of them pounded after me, ran me down halfway to the house and dragged me back to the bunkhouse wall. This time, without a word, the deputy handcuffed me to the hitching rail.

We waited.

Apparently unable to think of anything more appropriate, the marshal finally gave the command for another barrage of tear gas. The men fired, the grenades arched through the air and smashed against wall and doors and window shutters, obscuring the house with dust and smoke.

Before the gas cleared away the marshal came out of hiding—he was a brave little man—and trotted toward the house with the ax. Halfway there a fistful of dust spurted up at his feet, the bullet caromed off the ground and droned through the air. The marshal halted, staring at the house, his hat back, the ax hanging in his hand. The rifle spoke again, the bullet wanged past the marshal's shoulder. He turned and lumbered back to shelter, swearing, his belly jiggling.

"Kill them, Grandfather!" I hollered. "Kill them! What are you waiting for?" Why was he shooting all around them—had the gas blinded him? Tears were blinding me. I struggled with my handcuffs, shook the rail, and kicked at the deputy when he tried to stop me.

The marshal took out his frustration on me. "Put that kid in the car," he bellowed, "and take him clean away from here!"

The deputy came toward me.

"The rest of you," the marshal roared, turning to the others, "forget them grenades. Pump a few tracers into that house. Maybe we can burn that old lunatic outa there!"

At that moment the hum of a motor reached our ears. We all heard it. The deputy coming toward me hesitated, the marshal closed his mouth, the men stared up the slope toward the top of the ridge, where the road wound among the boulders.

The sun flashed on the glass of the big cream-colored automobile as it appeared over the top and came racing down the roar at a suicidal speed. It jounced along to the bottom, churning up plumes of dust, skidded around the turn beyond the pasture fence, and came rocking toward us under the grove of trees. Beside Lee, in the front seat, was the pale face, the big staring eyes, of a frightened woman. For one panic-struck moment I thought it was my mother—then I recognized her as Marian, my Alamogordo aunt.

Lee drove the car roughly into the clear space between the ranch-house and the besiegers, jammed on the brakes and jumped out, while the dust swirled wildly around the car and the screech of rubber sliding over rock still hung in the air.

He looked quickly around, standing bold and tall in the light and the sudden shocking silence.

"Lee!" I called.

He saw me, the terrible look of danger burned on his face. "Turn that boy loose!" he commanded.

Hurriedly the deputy released me. My Aunt Marian was out of the car by now and when she saw me came running toward me awkwardly, as women do, with her arms extended and tears streaming down her face. She hugged me to her, held me so tight and close I could barely breathe and could not see what Lee would do next. But I wasn't worried any more, the fear was washed away, and with it the outrage I'd felt while waiting for Lee to come.

"Oh you poor boy, you poor poor poor little boy," she cried over me. "What are you doing here? Why aren't you out of this? Why did he let you stay?" She kept embracing me and kissing me, closing my eyes with kisses. I had to break loose.

"Please," I said, "please, Grandfather is in there. Let's—please, let me see!"

Now Lee was talking to the marshal, his face taut with anger. But he spoke so quietly I couldn't hear what he said. Abruptly, harshly, he turned his back on the marshal and started walking toward the front of the house. In his hand he held the ax.

"John," he shouted. "It's time to quit. Let me in. This is Lee. Are you all right?"

From inside came Grandfather's voice, strangely muffled. "Stand back, Lee. Stand back."

"I'm coming in, old horse, don't try and stop me."

Lee walked steadily toward the porch, his hat back, the blade of the ax glittering before his hand.

"Stop, Lee," cried the old man from somewhere inside. "You stop now, Lee."

"I'm not stopping. Go ahead and shoot."

The old man fired over Lee's head. The bullet wailed through the air, cutting a few more leaves from the cottonwoods.

"Stop, Lee. Stand back now."

Lee kept walking. "No I won't stop, you old fool. You come out of there."

We heard the clatter of falling boards. The front door was opening violently from the inside and my grandfather appeared in the doorway, pointing the carbine straight at Lee.

"You stop. You stop, Lee—what do you think you're doing?"

Lee was now almost at the porch steps. "Shoot, old horse," he said. "Go ahead and shoot me." He dropped the ax.

Grandfather raised the muzzle of his gun and fired again, close over Lee's head. The report had hardly died away before he levered another shell into the chamber.

"Last time, Lee. Last time. You touch my house and I'll kill you."

Lee appeared to hesitate for a moment. He almost stopped. Then he said, "Go ahead," and stepped up on the verandah, coming within eight feet of the old man, who aimed the rifle directly at Lee's belly.

"I'll kill you!" the old man shouted.

"Here I am," Lee said. He stopped and opened his arms. "Here I am."

My grandfather paused. In the shade of the verandah we could see his whole body tremble, his face blanched pale with hatred and exasperation and defeat.

"You traitor!" he bellowed. "Oh, Lee, you dirty traitor!" And he threw the rifle as hard as he could down on the floor of the porch. His knees started to buckle.

Lee caught him before he fell and helped him walk toward us, toward Aunt Marian and me and the car that would take him away from the ranch.

I thought that Grandfather was weeping: his shoulders heaved, his head was down, his hands were clenching and unclenching in pain, but his eyes, when I saw them, were burned dry. He looked like a blind man.

Lee and Marian helped him into the back seat of the car. I stared at the old man.

Lee put his strong hand on my shoulder. "He'll be all right, Billy. Come on now."

I shook off his hand and glared up at him. "Keep your hand off me, Lee Mackie. Don't you ever talk to me again."

10

Three days later the old man disappeared.

We were staying with Aunt Marian in Alamorgordo, Grandfather and I, sleeping in her guest room, eating at her table. I was scheduled to leave for the East on the following day; Grandfather wasn't supposed to be going anywhere. But he went. He vanished. And I saw him go.

That first day and night after we separated him from his ranch he was a sick man. He would not speak to anyone, he would not look at anyone. He simply sat on a chair or lay on his bed, eyes wide open, staring at nothing.

Aunt Marian called in a doctor and the doctor treated the old man's eyes, which had been hurt but not seriously burned by the tear gas. He gave Grandfather a going-over with his instruments and said he could find nothing wrong except a temporary condition of what he called nervous shock. He prescribed sedative pills and plenty of rest.

Grandfather seemed to improve a little the next day. He ate a light meal, sat outside in the shade during the afternoon watching the neighbors ride their gasoline-powered lawn mowers over their tiny patches of lawn, and spoke a few words to me and my aunt. He wanted to know if the horses had been provided for.

She told him that the horses were all right, that Lee was keeping them on his place east of the city. The old man had to repeat his question; the almost continual roar of jet planes overhead was making conversation difficult. My aunt repeated her answer, and the old man said nothing more. I don't think he slept much that second night: he woke me up twice with his mumbling and getting out of bed to wander through the house.

The third night he left us. Soon after we were all in bed and the lights were out and the house was silent except for the mutter of the appliances and the braying of the traffic uptown and the thunder of jets above, he crawled out of his bunk, dressed himself in the dark, and padded across the room to me. He must've been feeling much better, in his way: a cigar was burning in his hand.

"You awake, Billy?"

"Yes sir."

He sat down on the edge of my bed and put his huge gentle hand on my shoulder. For a while he said nothing, just puffed on the cigar. At last he spoke:

"Billy, you remember that ride you and me and Lee took up to the mountain last June?"

"Sure, Grandfather. I'll never forget it."

"Remember how thirsty you got and how we kidded you about the canteen?"

"Yes."

"Did you ever tell Lee?"

"Tell him what, Grandfather?"

"That I was packing a canteen in my saddlebags?"

I thought for a moment. "No, I don't think I ever did. No sir, I'm sure I never told him—you asked me not to."

"That's right. And you never told him?"

"No sir."

His cigar flared up a little in the dark and then died down. I could see him fairly well by that time, as my eyes got used to the dim light coming in through the curtains and blinds. The old man was wearing his hat.

"I'm leaving here, Billy."

"I know, Grandfather."

"How did you know?"

I paused. "I can't—I don't know why. I just knew it."

"All right. Well, that's what I'm doing. I'm leaving. I'm running away tonight, just like a kid." He was silent. "No sir, I can't stay here another day. I have to pull out. Now I want to ask you this: Do you know where I'm gonna be?"

"Sir?"

"I'm going to hide, Billy, and I think you know where I'm going to do it. Don't you?"

I thought that over for a moment."Yes sir."

"Sure you do. I knew you would. But we won't mention it because when they all get on you—Marian and Lee and maybe Isabel will be here too, or your mother —when they start putting the pressure on you, why you can say I never told you where I was going. You won't have to lie too much. Do you follow, Billy?"

"Yes sir."

"That's good. And you promise not to tell them?"

"I promise, Grandfather."

"Fine. That's the idea." He started to rise from my bed.

"Let me go with you."

"What?"

"I want to go with you, Grandfather."

He puffed on the cigar. "No, Billy. That we can't do and you know it. You have to go home now. Maybe next summer—

"Home?"

"Yes. What'd I say? But next summer, maybe, you can join me again. We'll see how things work out."

"I wish I could go with you."

"I know. But this time I have to go by myself." He stood up slowly; I heard him sighing as he looked down at me.

"Goodbye, Billy."

I couldn't answer him; I was afraid to say goodbye and I was glad he could not see my tears. In the darkness I watched his tall figure turn, saw him take a small bundle off the dresser by his bed and move to the bedroom door. He faded away, stepping quietly down the hall and out the front door. Listening intently, I heard the sound of the pickup truck as he started the engine and drove off.

It took me a long time to get to sleep that night. And when I did sleep I was troubled by a dream: a dream of fireflies, of marvelous blue-flaming stars that kept receding from me, of a pair of yellow eyes burning in dusk and silence.

The excitement began the next morning when I walked into the kitchen for breakfast. My Aunt Marian and her husband were sitting there drinking coffee.

"Where's your grandfather?" she asked.

"He's okay."

"Somebody stole his truck last night," her husband said. "But don't get excited," he added, as I seemed to hesitate. "Don't tell the old man; he might get upset. I've already called the police about it. They'll probably find the truck before the day is over." He finished his coffee as I sat down at my place. "I told him several times he shouldn't leave the keys in the ignition. It's a bad habit which he's got to learn to break if he's going to live in town." He folded the newspaper and got up from the table. "I'll see you at dinner-time—and for godsake don't let the old man worry about the truck. I wonder if he has insurance on it? Oh well—I'd better go." And he rushed off to work.

My aunt set a bowl of hot cereal before me. "Isn't your grandfather going to have breakfast with us?"

"I don't think so," I said.

"Is he all right?"

"Sure he is."

"I think I'll have a look."

"He's sleeping."

"I won't wake him up, Billy," She walked out of the kitchen and down the hall to the bedrooms. I stirred a spoon in the cereal and braced myself for the scream. She didn't scream but when she returned a minute later she looked pale and awfully serious. She gripped my forearm and gave me her sternest look, right in the eyes. "Where is he?"

"I don't know."

"Don't lie to me, Billy. Where is he?"

"I don't know."

"You knew he wasn't there, didn't you? You knew he was gone."

"Yes."

"Then where did he go?"

"I don't know. He didn't tell me."

She went to the telephone. She called her husband's office, she called the city police and the country sheriff and the state police, and she called Lee Mackie:

"He's disappeared. What? . . . No, we don't know . . . We don't know when—sometime last night . . . Yes, in the truck . . . Who? . . . Yes, he's here. . . . But he won't talk. . . . He says he doesn't know. . . . Yes, that's what I think. . . . Yes, we notified the police. . . . Can you come over? . . . We'll be here. . . . That's good. . . . Yes. . . . See you then."

An hour later the State Police called and informed Aunt Marian that the pickup truck belonging to John Vogelin had been fund in El Paso, abandoned in an alley and stripped of its tires and other parts. Soon afterwards Lee arrived.

"Why on earth would he go to El Paso?" he asked me.

"I don't want to talk to you."

"Billy!" my aunt said. "You could at least be polite."

"Yes, ma'am."

"That's better."

"Why would he go to El Paso?" Lee insisted.

"I don't know. He didn't tell me where he was going." I stared at the table top and wished they would both go away.

"I wonder if it's a trick," Lee muttered. He put his hand on my shoulder. I shook it off and slid my chair farther away from him. "Look here, Billy," he said, watching me severely. "Your grandfather is not well.

He may be very sick. If you know where he went you'd better tell us."

"I don't know."

"He might need help. He might be in trouble."

I was silent. Lee and my aunt stared at me, grimly, until I had to turn my head away and look somewhere else. I looked out the window at the neighbor's wall and forsythia bush, through the neighbor's window at his television set.

"Does the old man have friends in El Paso?" Lee asked my Aunt Marian. "Can you think of any reason why he would get up in the middle of the night to go there?"

"No, I can't. I suppose he knows people down there but I don't know who."

"Did he take money with him?"

"I don't know. He left almost all of his clothes and things here."

Lee looked at me. "When's this boy supposed to fly home?"

"Tomorrow."

"Well, keep an eye on him. Don't let *him* sneak away."

"Don't worry about that."

Promising to return after lunch if Grandfather failed to appear, Lee put on his hat and left us. My aunt put in a long-distance call to her sister in Phoenix and told her what had happened. She made some effort to do her housekeeping while we waited, and prepared a lunch for the two of us as the morning passed on to noon. She would not let me out of her sight.

Late in the afternoon Lee came back.

"Any word?" he asked Aunt Marian.

"Nothing."

"Anything from El Paso?"

"Not a word."

"You called them?"

"Lee, I've been calling the police and the sheriff's

office about every half hour. Nobody has seen a trace of him."

Lee sat down at the kitchen table with us, removing his hat. He ran his hand through his thick black hair and turned his dark eyes on me. Unsmiling. "Marian," he said, watching me, "I cannot understand why he would go to El Paso. Nobody can understand it. There doesn't seem to be any reason for it."

"There's no reason for his leaving my house in the middle of the night without even saying goodbye."

"I know. It's strange. We have to try to guess what was going on in his head. Maybe we can reconstruct what happened. If the boy here will help us a little."

"Stop staring at me," I said, "I don't know where he went."

"Didn't he go to El Paso?"

I hesitated. "I don't know. I guess he did."

"How did his truck get there if he didn't go there? It didn't drive itself. You didn't drive it. How did it get there, Billy?"

"I don't know, I tell you."

"Billy, don't you yell at Lee."

"Yes, ma'am."

Lee kept looking at me all the time. "You know," he said, speaking to Marian, "when you called me up this morning, my first idea was: I bet that old horse thief went back to the ranch. That's the first thing I thought of. So I called the marshal and I called the Air Force Police. I thought they might be having another war out there. But no, they said everything was quiet—nobody had gone out that way last night or this morning."

I smiled. Too late I raised my hand to cover the smile. They pounced on me like a pair of FBI agents.

"Billy!"

"Did he go out there, Billy?"

I paused, glowering back at them. They had me cornered. "All right," I said. "I'll tell you the truth. He said he was going to Old Mexico."

They stared at me. "Is that the truth, Billy?"

"He said he was sick of this country."

They were silent for a moment. Then Lee reached out and tried to put his hand on mine. I pulled my hand away. "Billy," he said, peering into my eyes, "I think you are the biggest liar that ever hit Guadalupe County."

I said nothing.

"I think you are the biggest liar in southeast New Mexico," he went on. "Maybe in the whole state—outside of Santa Fe." He paused. "I think I'll take a ride out to the ranch."

"I want to go too," I said at once.

For the first time that day he smiled. "Get your hat."

"I'm going too," Aunt Marian said.

"No, you're not," Lee said. "This is a job for men. Get your hat, Billy." And we left her there to wash the dishes.

As we climbed into Lee's big car, he said: "Maybe we ought to trade this for a jeep. What do you think, Billy?"

"What for?" I said sullenly.

He looked at me in a careful way. "Because I think your grandfather is up on the mountain."

I stared bitterly out of the window as we drove up the street. "Why can't you let him alone?"

"Billy, I just want to make sure the old man is all right. We're not going to kidnap him. If he wants to stay there we'll let him stay there." He tried to touch me again; this time I let his hand rest on my arm. "Does that make you feel better?" he asked.

I did not reply. I did not feel any better, I felt worse. I felt like a betrayer. A traitor.

Forty-five minutes later we were barreling south on the highway in a rented jeep, bound for Baker and the old man's ranch. When we reached the village Lee stopped in at Hayduke's place and the Wagon Wheel Bar to make inquiries: everybody knew that grandfather was missing but no one had seen him. We got back in the jeep and turned west over the familiar dirt road. Lee inspected the road for tracks—there were too many. "Looks like an army's been out this way today," he said.

We drove on under the grand clear desert sky. The sun burned along its high summer track, drifting towards evening, the dunes shimmered with heat and the bright white salt flats glittered like frosted glass, painful to look at. Lee put on a pair of sunglasses.

"What are those?" I asked.

"Sunglasses. What do they look like?"

"They look like hell."

"Things change, Billy. Even the Indians wear them now. Why don't you stop fighting the world and get in step? I mean—there must be a better way of saying it."

"Keep trying."

"You try them." He handed the dark glasses to me and I put them on. To my surprise the sky looked bluer, the sand a deeper shade of tan, the yucca blades a more interesting green. Something wrong here, I thought; I don't understand this. Silently I gave the sunglasses back to Lee.

"They work, huh Billy? You have to admit they work, they even make thinks look prettier." He grinned at me. "We have to be smart like the other Indians, Billy. We don't take everything the white man tries to dump on us but we make choices, we take what we can use and we let him bury himself with the rest. You understand?"

I nodded. I did not understand but I thought I could see a few dim tracks.

"Whoa!" Lee shouted. He slowed the jeep, stopped, backed it through our trailing cloud of dust. "Did you see what I saw?"

"No," I said.

He stopped the jeep again and looked over the ground to our right: perfectly parallel and fresh, the twin imprints of rubber tires veered off the road over the rocks, through the sand, and twisted among the shrubs of creosote brush and mesquite toward the northwest.

"Why would anybody drive out there?" Lee asked. "I'll tell you why: to get around the guards up ahead, that's why. Your grandfather drove this far, remembered the guards at the gate, and decided to detour around them. Like you did when you walked this road."

"Are you going to follow the tracks?"

"What for? We know his destination. We're going straight to the cabin."

"But—if the truck's in El Paso?"

Lee started the jeep forward. "Oh, he's real tricky, your grandfather. He probably picked up some wetback or soldier in Alamogordo and made a deal, maybe paid him something to bring him out to the hills and then told him he could keep the truck. Whoever got the truck would naturally drive it to the big city to strip it and sell the parts."

"Why not hide the truck out in the mountains?"

"Because he wanted to steer us way off his tracks. Don't you see? Real tricky. There's only one thing now I can't figure out."

"What's that?"

He grinned at me through the dust. "How he thought he could fool me."

He trusted you, I thought. But I didn't speak it aloud —I was guilty too.

Reading my thoughts again, he squeezed my shoulder. "Stop your brooding, Billy. We can both keep a secret. We won't let him down."

"What about Aunt Marian?"

He paused. "Yeah . . . that could be a problem. Well —if we have to we'll lie to her, that's all. Can you tell a lie as well as you can keep a secret?"

"I guess I'm not much good at either."

"You'll improve. At both."

The Air Police halted us when we reached the gate; Lee produced the pass he'd been using for the past couple of weeks.

"This pass is no good any more," the guard said. "Vogelin doesn't live here now, Mr. Mackie, you know that. What's your business today?"

Lee wasn't quite ready for the question. "We're looking for a horse," I said.

"That's right," Lee said. "An old horse."

The guard eyed us warily. "Okay, Mr. Mackie, we'll let you through this time. You promise to come out again before sundown?"

"Yes, sure. Thanks a lot."

"That's all right, Mr. Mackie. Just be sure you're out by dark."

We drove on through. "Great to live in a free country," Lee said, "with well-trained and courteous cops everywhere you go. Now keep your eyeballs skinned and we'll see where the old man came back on the road."

But we didn't.

"Well, he decided not to take any chances, that's all," Lee explained. "I guess he drove clean around the ranch. Don't worry, we'll find him."

That's what I was worried about.

As we crossed the ancient lakebed where the loading pens were—empty corrals, abandoned now to the weather and the bombing practice: they'd make satisfactory targets—we saw a funnel of dust boiling up from the other side of the basin and at its forward tip a gray government sedan, speeding toward us.

The driver of the car flagged us down. We stopped side by side on the road and Mr. Burr leaned head and elbow out of his window to talk to Lee. The marshal was alone this time. "Where are you two going?" he asked; his tone and his expression were hostile.

"We thought the old man might be at the ranch," Lee said.

"I told you this morning there wasn't anybody out here."

"I see." Lee fingered the dust on his jaw. "I thought he might possibly show up this evening."

"It won't do him any good. If he does you better bring him out again."

"That's why I came."

The marshal looked at our jeep, at me, at Lee's hard brown face. "You're not allowed in here after sunset," he said.

"We'll be out."

The marshal considered us once more with his insolent, lazy, lizard eyes, withdrew into his steel shell and drove off. We continued on our way, while I looked back to make sure the marshal didn't turn around and follow us. Lee also was glancing at the rear-view mirror.

"You think he might try to follow us, Lee?"

"I was thinking of that. But he'd have a hard time getting that car across the Salado. And even if he made that he couldn't drive it very far up the trail road."

"He could walk."

"He's too fat and lazy. It'd kill him."

"I hope he tries then."

"I know how you feel, Billy. I sure hated to have to be so polite with that—toad. I could've killed him the other day. I *would've* killed him if he'd hurt John."

We topped out on the ridge above the ranch buildings, stopped and looked down. There was no sign of human life below—no smoke in the chimney, no light in the window, no pickup truck or car in the yard under the cottonwoods. Even the dogs and chickens were gone, as well as the horses and the milk cow. The only movement we perceived down there was the slow turning of the windmill as it continued to pump water into the tank and from there into the ditches that watered the garden and filled the trough in the corral and carried whatever surplus remained to the pasture beyond the corral. And while we watched, the breeze died, the gray vanes slowed their whirling, paused and waited. The whole place became still, silent, dead.

"This was a man's home," Lee murmured. "This was home for a dozen different people and their children and animals. Now it all goes back to the spiders and the rattlesnakes. And the Government." He looked up: the sun was getting closer to the western mountains. "Let's go, Billy."

We drove down the hill, down to the ranch, and through gates left open that didn't have to be closed anymore right up to the edge of the Salado wash. Lee shifted into fourwheel drive, we dropped into the sand and stormed across through the sand and over the dry streambed and up the bank on the far side. The pale leaves of the cottonwoods twinkled above our heads with a dry rustling noise that seemed meaningless now. A pair of ravens roosting on a dead limb croaked like wizards when we passed. We began the journey to the mountains.

"I see jeep tracks all over the place," Lee said. "You'd think the Army was having maneuvers out here. If the old man cut back this way we won't find his sign now." He drove as fast as he could over the rocky trail, through pockets of sand and in and out of deepening arroyos, straight toward the glare of the sinking sun.

We approached a scene along the road that looked familiar yet uncomfortably changed: a certain arrangement of bushes, rocks, a curve in the ruts—the bristling bayonets of a giant yucca. An instant later I recognized the place and realized, as we passed, what was wrong: the great twelve-foot stalk of the yucca, with its cluster of dry seed pods at the tip, now lay prone on the sand, hacked down by somebody with a big knife or machete. I said nothing to Lee. We bounced and rattled on, trailing a plume of dust that hung in the air for half a mile, golden in the evening sunlight, obscuring our view to the rear.

Down into the ravine and up the other side: another windmill appeared, standing up against the sky, with its water tank, corral, loading chute. No cattle, no horses, waited for us there now. Hot, dusty, thirsty though we were, Lee drove by without slackening his speed, past the mouth of the canyon and up the narrow wagon road into the foothills.

"I'm not even looking for his tracks now," Lee yelled at me through the noise. "I feel so sure he's up there." He gestured toward the peak of Thieves' Mountain.

The engine groaned as the pitch grew steeper, the rear wheels spun on the loose stones, and the back of the jeep swung toward the edge of the drop-off. Again Lee had to stop and engage the front axle; with four wheels pulling we ground up into the canyon pine and juniper, over the burnt flowerless weeds of August, pursuing shadowy birds which fled before the clamor of the machine. We passed the south ridge trail, drove beyond the point where Lee and I had routed the Army, and finally reached the junction of the old mine road and the wagon trail. But there we had to stop: several felled pine trees blocked the way that led up to the cabin.

Lee nudged the jeep against the first log and shut off the motor. "I guess we walk from here on up, old buddy."

We climbed out, stretched our limbs, listened to the quiet stirring of the trees, the dim bird cries, and looked at the barricaded trail. "He doesn't want visitors," Lee said. "Not on wheels, at any rate." He looked around. "My God, it's quiet up here now. Remember how lively it seemed last June?"

"I remember." I looked to the north: far out that way, past several fields in the mountain, my mind came to the awful spot where Grandfather and I had found the lost pony with his head broken, his belly ripped open, the vultures feeding on his entrails. "Let's get up there to the cabin," I said. "Maybe we better hurry."

"Listen!"

I was still. A tree limb creaked, a few pinyon jays screeched below. And I heard the drone of an engine coming up the mountain. "My God!" I said. "He followed us."

"Sounds like a jeep," Lee said, cocking his head. "It is a jeep. Maybe it's not the marshal at all."

"Those Air Police had a jeep."

"Yes. Well, there's nothing we can do about it now. Let's go up to the cabin."

"But—we don't want to—" I hesitated.

"Come on. It'll be all right."

I wasn't sure about that but when Lee climbed over the fallen trees and started marching up the trail I went after him. As we climbed, the sun went down behind the mountain peak and the vast shadow covered us, covered the fear in my heart. We walked up the road through a filtered twilight, cool and gloomy, with the pine boughs whispering over our heads. A huge bird with long dark wings flopped off a limb and sailed away: the limb rose up, trembling.

"What was that?"

"What, Billy?"

"That bird."

"I didn't see it. I was watching the road. I think your grandfather walked up here last night. Or early this morning. See this bootprint? That's him."

We climbed faster, breathing hard and not talking much. Every now and then the noise of the jeep floated up from the hills below, coming closer.

At last we reached the end of the road and saw before us the level park of waving gramma grass, the corral, and the cabin set against the cliffs which rose up and up toward the summit of the mountain. We stopped for a moment to rest, to catch up with our breathing, and started toward the cabin. A man sat against the wall near the open door, hatless, facing us but with his head bowed, looking at the ground between his legs. He did not see us.

"Grandfather!" I shouted, waving my hand. There was no response. Was it really the old man? At that distance, with the glow of the sunset in our eyes, I could not be certain. I called again: "Grandfather?"

The only reply came from the mountain, as the cliffs

echoed my voice. We hurried forward, staring at the man who sat by the cabin door, completely unaware of our approach.

"Hey, John," Lee said, as we came close, "are you all right?"

Grandfather did not lift his head. He made no move. He sat in a strange, slumping, boneless way, supported by the wall, his hands resting on the ground, his glasses missing, his eyes half open and gazing blindly at the earth between his sprawled legs. His hat lay on the grass nearby, where it had fallen.

We stood awkwardly in front of him. "Grandfather?" I said softly.

A fly buzzed near the old man's face and a faint, queer odor hovered in the twilight. I squatted down, looking into his eyes. The eyes I looked at could not look back at me. I reached out to touch him but my hand stopped of its own volition before I made contact. I willed the hand to move forward but it seemed to be paralyzed. I was unable to make myself touch the old man's body.

Lee took off his hat and brushed the sweat from his forehead. He dropped the hat, put his hand on my shoulders and drew me back. "Your grandfather's dead, Billy." He stepped past me, put his arms under the old man's back and laid him gently out on the ground. He closed the eyelids, picked up the salt-rimed old hat and placed it on Grandfather's chest.

"He's been dead for hours, Billy."

I shook my head unable to speak, and backed away a few steps, staring at the old man. *No*, I thought, but I could not say it.

"Too much for him," Lee said quietly. "Seventy years—too much trouble. Hiking up this mountain last night, chopping down those trees—oh the goddamned old fool. . . ." And Lee, kneeling on the ground beside the body, lowered his head, put his hands over his face and began to cry. "Oh the old fool—why did he do this? —damned crazy stubborn old. . . ." His head sank lower, his back shuddered in an uncontrolled spasm of sobs.

The sight of Lee Mackie bent double with grief, the awful sound of his weeping, somehow seemed to me more shocking than the death of the old man. I backed off further and turned away, stared out over the hills, watched the shadow of the mountain advance like a wing over the brilliant golden light on the desert. I too wanted to weep, to wail like a child, but I couldn't do it. I felt only a cold stillness in my nerves, a dark and nameless anger. I envied Lee and his tears, realizing at last that he was closer to the old man and loved him more than I ever had.

After a while Lee stopped crying, got up off his knees and came to me. He put his arm around my shoulders and together we looked out at the light on the plain. Far off to the northeast we could see the first tiny lights of Alamogordo appear, the flash of a beacon on the mountains beyond the city. "Getting dark, Billy. We better take him down."

"Take him down?"

"We can't leave him here. The wild beasts will tear him to pieces. We'll have to carry him down to the jeep."

"But wait—" I hesitated. "Why—let's bury him here."

"We can't do that. We can't do that, Billy. People will have to see him. The coroner, the undertaker. Your aunts will want to see him, other relatives. . . . You know how they do this thing now, Billy."

I was silent.

"Even if we wanted to, we couldn't bury him here. Six inches down we'd hit nothing but granite."

"He wanted to be here, Lee."

"I know that." Lee said nothing for a few moments. "We shouldn't do it," he said.

"We could cover the body with rocks. Isn't that what they used to do?"

"Rocks," Lee muttered, "rocks." He looked around. "But they could roll off the rocks, take him away." He rubbed his jaw in thought, his eyes shone as he searched the field, the corrals and cabin, the edge of the woods, the lavender evening, seeking an idea. His glance went to the cabin. "*Yes*. Here's what we'll do, Billy. We'll cremate the body. We'll give him a fire, the biggest funeral fire you ever saw in your life. That's it—we'll put the old man inside, inside the cabin, on the bunk in there, and we'll set fire to the cabin. Why not? We'll launch him off to the stars like a Viking. He'd like that —his name's Vogelin, isn't it?"

And Lee went to work. Tenderly he picked up the old man's body and carried it into the cabin. He laid him on the cot and dragged the cot to the center of the floor, shoving the table aside. But then he hesitated again and stopped. Thrusting his fingers through his tangled hair, he gaped at me in doubt:

"Billy—what are we doing? Do you realize what we're doing? We can't ever tell anyone about this."

I stood inside the doorway, watching. "Why not?"

"It's against the law. We could get into all kinds of trouble. They might even think—Look, Billy, you must never tell anybody about this. Do you understand?"

"Yes, Lee."

"This is a secret between you and me. For the rest of our lives. Agreed?"

"I agree."

"Okay. Now let's take the kerosene out of this lamp—"

"Hold on there!" another voice spoke sharply. Marshal Burr stood in the doorway, frowning at us, wiping the sweat from his face. "What are you fellas doing here?" He looked at the body laid out on the cot, the closed eyes, the folded hands, the hat placed like a wreath on the old man's chest. "Say, what's—what's going on here anyway?" He stared at Grandfather. "What happened?"

Lee said, "You can see. He died. Died of heartbreak. We found him here when we came up."

The marshal came into the cabin, staring suspiciously at the body of the old man. He stepped beside him and picked up Grandfather's wrist and held it. At the same time he bent down, taking off his hat, and put one ear to grandfather's mouth. After a minute, satisfied, he replaced the hand as we had arranged it and turned toward us. "Very sorry this had to happen. Very sorry." He looked sternly at Lee and slapped the hat back on "It's too late to get anybody out here this evening. But I'll notify the county sheriff and he'll get the coroner and an undertaker out here first thing in the morning." He looked about. "I suggest we close up this cabin tight to keep the varmints out. What was he doing here?"

Quietly I unscrewed the burner from the fuel bowl of the lamp.

"I guess he came back here to die," Lee said.

"You knew he was here?"

"Yes."

"Why didn't you tell me?"

Lee paused. "I didn't want to see you and DeSalius and all your dirty-fingered military cops hounding this old man any more. Now get out of here before I lose my patience and kick your ribs in."

Mr. Burr paled a bit and backed carefully to the doorway, his hands raised and alert, his eyes intent on Lee. I judged the time had come to pour the kerosene.

"You're talking to a United States Marshal; you're threatening an officer of the law."

"I know it. Don't irritate me."

The pool of kerosene spread over the floor under the table and chairs, soaking into the aged, dried-out boards. I took matches from the box on the stove.

"What's that boy doing?"

"We're going to cremate the old man's body," Lee said. "I advise you to step outside if you want to watch. Strike a match, Billy."

I struck a fistful of matches and dropped them on the spreading stain. Instantly the yellow flames sprang up, lapping at the furniture and reaching toward the wall.

"You two must be crazed," the marshal said. "You can't do this. It's illegal. We don't even have a death certificate." He came in again, moving toward the body on the cot.

Lee picked up a chair and raised it over his head. "Don't you touch him."

The marshal stopped. I pulled ancient yellowed newspapers out of the cupboard shelves, spilling tin dishes to the floor, wadded the papers and threw them on the fire. They billowed up in flame, curling around the table legs.

"You can't do this," the marshal shouted. "It's against the law." Again he made a tentative move toward the old man.

"Stand back," Lee hollered, "or I'll brain you."

The fire began to grow along the edge of the floor, eating at the warped and exposed board ends. A few flames flickered up the wall and touched the shelving. Smoke gathered under the rafters. I stepped toward the doorway.

"Get out of here, Billy," Lee said. "I'll hold him off."

I edged around the marshal and reached the doorway. The light of the fire made the world outside seem dark as night already.

"I can't let you do this!" the marshal shouted at Lee. "You can't dispose of a body this way. And this cabin is now Government property. You're wilfully destroying Goverment property."

Lee smashed the chair in the table top. He kept one leg of the chair clutched in his right hand and pushed the other pieces onto the fire. Holding the chair leg like a club, he stood against Grandfather's bier and faced the marshal. I could see the light of the flames in his eyes.

"I'm going to file charges against you," Mr. Burr yelled. "You're going to regret this."

Lee grinned at him, holding the club aloft. The fire

crept around him over the floor, licked at the mattress on the cot, grew bigger under the table and broken wood, filled the cabin with smoke.

The marshal backed toward the door as the heat became unpleasant. "This is going to hurt you," he howled at Lee; "You're going to have the record against you for the rest of your life."

Lee grinned at the man again, squinting through the smoke. The marshal cursed, turned abruptly and marched out of the doorway, pushing me to one side. His eyes were red with fury and the sweat poured down his face. Lee came outside and stood beside me as we watched him stomping across the field, fading into the twilight.

The table collapsed inside, one leg eaten away, and the fire rose up with added vigor. We faced the cabin, staring at the flames, and waited. Waited till the whole interior of the cabin became a seething inferno moaning like the wind, and bits and pieces and sections of the roof began to fall in. Grandfather on his bunk disappeared within the fire, wrapped from head to foot in flame, and cell by cell, atom by atom, he rejoined the elements of earth and sky.

The fire now seemed the brightest thing in the world as evening covered the mountains and desert and the first few stars emerged from the sky. Far away to the northeast and to the south the light of Alamogordo and El Paso twinkled like tiny beds of jewels in the velvet dark. If anyone out there cared to look, he'd see our funeral bonfire flickering like a signal, like an alarm, high on the side of the mountain of thieves.

The fire burst through the roof and streamed around the walls of the cabin, flaring wild and magnificent in the darkness, blazing with angry heat. Lee and I stepped back, our faces hot. He squeezed my shoulder and smiled at me, that foolish and generous smile, his face grimy with dust, sweat and smoke.

"The old man would like this, Billy. He'd approve of this."

The walls crackled and crashed, forcing us still further back. We stared in awe as the fire achieved the climax of its energy and towered above the cabin, rolling up and up in a pillar of smoke and sparks and flames that illuminated for one moment of splendor the entire height of the granite cliffs beyond the rim.

Far above on the mountainside, posed on his lookout point, troubled by the fire, the lion screamed.

Jay Dusard

ABOUT THE AUTHOR

EDWARD ABBEY (1927–1989) was a provocative novelist, essayist, naturalist, philosopher, and social critic, and one of the most popular writers from the American West. In addition to *Fire on the Mountain*, he is the author of *The Monkey Wrench Gang; Desert Solitaire; The Fool's Progress; One Life at a Time, Please; The Brave Cowboy;* and others.